WALKING FORWARD, LOOKING BACK

WALKING FORWARD, LOOKING BACK

A DISTRICT NURSE'S LIFE JOURNEY

DINAH LATHAM

Matador
9 Priory Business Park
Kibworth Beauchamp
Leicestershire LE8 0RX, UK
Tel: (+44) 116 279 2299
Fax: (+44) 116 279 2277
Email: books@troubador.co.uk
Web: www.troubador.co.uk/matador

ISBN 978-1784620-844

British Library Cataloguing in Publication Data.
A catalogue record for this book is available from the British Library.

Typeset in Aldine by Troubador Publishing Ltd
Printed and bound in the UK by TJ International, Padstow, Cornwall

Matador is an imprint of Troubador Publishing Ltd

CONTENTS

Illustrations   John Martin
Poem   Elke Dutton

FOREWORD

There was a small boy standing on a large beach. There had been a violent storm with rough seas that had thrown all the starfish right up to the very top of the beach, beyond the high tide line. The boy was surrounded by thousands of starfish, and one by one he was throwing them back into the sea. A passer-by said to him, "What are you doing? There are far too many of them. You can't possibly make a difference to all of those."

The little boy bent down and picked up another starfish and, as he threw it back into the sea, he said,

"But I can make a difference to this one."

PREFACE

I've heard it said that the life of every man is a diary. I love diaries… other people's real lives laid bare. Somehow I've never had the persistence to keep one of those daily records past the third week in January, just as my New Year resolutions begin to falter.

Yet I have begun to reflect on my life as I have found myself in a new and untried world: that of the dog walker. Translated, that means 'dog owner being walked by her dog', the journey being accompanied by many stops for dog to nose around, observe and explore, determined to leave no leaf unturned.

Quite why these hesitations have set my mind travelling backwards I'm not sure, but here I am, on a chilly morning with my dog by my side, randomly flicking through a lifetime of unwritten diaries. I'm bewildered as to style and presentation; how to record reflections that are unselective as to date, time or sequence, encouraged by discoveries whilst walking, maybe prompted by weather, season or something we've seen. How then will this indiscriminate panorama take on any discernable shape? It promises to be a narrative that reads more like dipping in and out of a bag of assorted sweets, never being quite sure what you will find in your hand each time or what the taste will be…

1

GOOD MORNING MR LION

I'm not sure what led me to get a dog but whatever my uncertainty was then, there is no doubt that it is she who is leading me now.

I had, in some distant past, cherished the idea of becoming a district nurse and midwife, which meant to me a home of my own where I could have a dog. In those days, in the early 1960s, the district nurse and midwife was a job undertaken by one person with both qualifications who was given a home to rent within the community she served. Indeed, as my career plan took shape, so it was to be… but instead of getting the dog, I got a husband. The husband, four children, a divorce and a long struggle working more than full-time hours for over twenty years meant that dog ownership had been pushed to the bottom of any wish list.

Nursing in the community brought me close to families at both the beginning and end of their lives. Caring for patients who are dying, where they and their families have chosen to have their last months and death at home, is always a contemplative time. Being closely involved with those who are facing impending death and reflecting on their lives meant that I often found myself considering what I would regret not having done, were I to be diagnosed with a life-threatening disease. Whenever I pondered this big question, what bubbled, almost incongruously, to the surface every time was sadness that I had never owned a dog. I disapproved of my thoughts and reproached myself that I couldn't come up with some more worthwhile regret, such as lamenting the fact that I'd never written a seminal text on the essence of nursing care or won 'the nurse of the year' award; but no, while I didn't understand it, what came up every time was sorrow at not having experienced befriending a dog.

So, being more aware than most that life's direction can turn on a sixpence, I set about making it happen at my first realistic opportunity which was when I retired. Being inexperienced, a novice, I read books and I talked to people – all of whom it seemed did their best to dissuade me, telling me what a bad idea it was.

"They're a terrible tie, you know."

"What happens if you get an awful, probably vicious, rescue dog?"

"What happens if you want to jet off to Paris for lunch with a lover in the freedom of your retirement?"

The latter possibility called for some thought... but not for long; there is a really good hotel and restaurant locally that serves the most fantastic crème brûlée. I understand they have four-poster beds (I've always dreamt of nights of rapturous passion in a four-poster bed) and I think they do unbelievably scrumptious croissants for breakfast too. Why would I want to fly to Paris?

It's perhaps doubtful that I'll have a need to book in frequently...

Sometimes fortune takes a paw. This point in my life came together with a very active dog with a joyful disposition. I had no notion then of the profound relationship that was to develop between us; the companionship that would add an unexpected richness to my life. This union may just have been the coming together of chance and good timing but destiny or happy accident, it was certainly a blessing. It was her need to be taken on long walks, and me sharing her twice daily sojourns, that allowed me to deliberate, to reflect and to make sense of my own life journey.

I discovered what an entirely changed experience it is walking with and without a dog. It's a completely different activity. To go for a walk with a dog that enjoys it so much compels one to enter into the event with the same amount of excitement and fervour: to tilt your nose high, to sniff in the freshness of a new day with front legs fully extended forwards over the front doorstep, leaving your back legs behind, stretched to their absolute limit and still inside the doorway, is enough to make anyone wag their tail. She greets every day with boundless enthusiasm and optimism wherever we go. As alarm clocks are going off all over town and as the thin, feeble sun inches above the skyline, we walk.

I was told she was thought to be a Bearded/Border Collie cross when I collected her from the rescue. However, since then, those who are in the know tell me that this is incorrect and that she is in fact a Working Beardie (rather than a Show Beardie). Whatever the breed, Harriet, the seven-week-old puppy, arrived to turn my life upside down. She was to make sure I wasn't going to vegetate in my retirement, to remind me of how much joy there is in every waking moment and to be sure to savour the wonder of a dandelion clock as it blows away in the wind… even when it lands on your nose and makes you sneeze.

And so it was that our walks, and my reflections, began.

★ ★ ★

We set off to our left, going first over to the quadrangle on North Road opposite our front door. Most days we hesitate outside the door, Harriet turning her head this way and that wondering which way we'll start off today. Neither of us really knows but there, pausing on the pavement outside our door, is our starting point and our daily beginning.

As we head along the road towards the common, Harriet increases her pace, encouraging me to pick up mine. I resist being asked to exaggerate my step rate too much. I know we're off on at least a two-hour trek and, even though I'm unsure quite where we'll walk to or which direction we'll return home from, I do know that deliberate rapid-type walking it is not. Anyway, her four paws are capable of a much greater pace than my two. This is a retired day when I am able to allow my mind to wander along with my feet in an unstructured, maybe even disordered, way. The deliciousness of that lack of severe organisation of thought, as well as the timekeeping that is needed when in the workplace, never escapes me as we start off in the mornings; so let's just go and see what happens.

I'm not sure about her mind, but certainly the route Harriet takes is disordered. It's all over the place once she's off the lead: first following her nose, then distracted by an interesting looking stick, followed by a gambol across the field with a snoopy looking dog friend, before returning to my feet, just to make sure I'm still coming, before she runs ahead again.

★ ★ ★

The last time I had walked regularly was all the way back with the daily walks, taking the children to and from school. More structured then, definite times for leaving, and we aimed for a good steady pace to make sure we got there on time. There would be Izzie in the pram – one of the old style, coach-built carriages, so well sprung that it bounced easily along the pavement with no effort – and the three boys, Jon, Ben and Matt, bobbing along on either side, either reciting their tables, knocking conkers out of the tree with a stick, carefully carrying the jar with the stickleback in it for the nature table, or dragging their satchel along the ground, while they dawdled behind, creeping unwillingly to school.

It was always a reflective time, the walk to and from school: sometimes busy with chatter, sometimes thoughtful with growing minds working out the ways of the world. Rain or shine, wind or frost, it was a good time; a precious time for sharing thoughts.

One happening was constant: over the lane it sloped rapidly away to our right, downhill to the riverbed, while we turned left and pushed the pram steadily up the hilly bit. Here we all gathered on the corner in readiness to cross the road to the pavement on the second leg of the journey. A large tree dominated this corner and it had a sawn off branch at the top, just where the trunk ended and the other branches began. The old, weathered, lopped off, cross-section surface of this would-be branch bore the clear image of a lion's face, created by its age rings. It became a morning ritual, repeated over many years, all raised faces and voices greeting him with:

"Good Morning, Mr Lion."

So here I am, many years later, on regular walks again but without either the children or Mr Lion; with no set destination and only Harriet and my thoughts for company.

The lack of the rigid schedule required when at work, allowing thoughts to wander, to reflect and to meander, is perhaps never encountered so acutely as in retirement. The rich tapestry of one's life billows out behind like the brightly coloured canopy of a hot air balloon as it prepares to launch. The sun streaks through its richly-coloured panels and we gather in our recollections, capturing them to store in our memory basket.

Knowing there are fewer years ahead of us than behind us perhaps encourages this luxury of reminiscence… a time to explore not just the relationships of our lives but the emotions entwined with all we have done, been and become.

I've begun to think about a lot of new beginnings as they've presented themselves to me now in this new life I'm leading. I've come into my pint-sized, ground floor flat, leaving my single parent, post-divorce home, to enable me financially to retire. Until now, either some or all of the grown-up children had returned, and returned again, to live at home following university, right up to the time I moved. So, alongside retirement, I was now beginning life alone. A whole new life of beginnings…

★ ★ ★

An earlyish walk today for Harriet and me: the air is crisp and fresh with the dew catching the weak, early morning sun across the rectory field. My fingers tingle. Harriet noses her way through the overgrown track and hesitates as the tracks cross, waiting to see which way we are going today. I choose to go along the brow of the hill and left across the cornfield, where we can look down over the rooftops in the valley. We continue down across the field and turn at the bottom to come up the hill the other side of the wide meadow. It gets steeper as we come to the edge of the woodland as it streaks up to the road. As we walk on, heading home through the high street, the hustle and bustle of the day is just beginning: people making their way to work but shops not open yet. Around the corner, we are greeted by a gathering of yellow-jacketed children. Laughter and chatter, lunch bags swung around shoulders, with high pitched screeches of "Hi Harriet!" Harriet's ears prick up and her tail wags, while lots of hands wave to her across the road. We wave and carry on travelling as the 'walking train' of yellow jackets turns away and sets off to school. I watch them go and find myself thinking about walking to my village school for the very first time.

★ ★ ★

It's difficult to remember my first day at school in context, without the memories of that day being affected by all that followed – the devastating despair of learning I was a failure.

"You're not as bright as your sisters, are you?"

"Do you *have* to write in that silly way with your left hand?"

I was to learn that, from this day forward, I would forever be known as 'the girl with the red hair'.

My absolute sinking feeling as 'The Problem' was written at the top of the blackboard on Monday morning and me knowing, right there and then, that I would never be able to work out how long it would take to fill a bath if one tap ran at half the speed of the other and the bath was deeper at one end than the other. Never in a million years, let alone find out by Friday… and not enough brain to see that it didn't matter anyway, and certainly not enough nerve to say so!

Nasty teachers, nasty ink that spilled all over the desk and me, a longing to be the blackboard monitor so I could rub the board clean at the end of each day (a dream never to be fulfilled) and years of working very hard running parallel with a total lack of achievement.

All this alters the reality of that first day at school which was really about a very happy, excited little girl who wanted to learn to read.

★ ★ ★

Harriet disappears into a thicket and I'm quite a way ahead before I realise she's not following. I turn to call her and she appears with, horror of horrors, something in her mouth. Her head is up, showing off her 'catch'! As she bounds towards me I'm deciding what action I'll take with her find, not sure whether I want it to be a mangy well dead offering or can I heroically rescue some injured bird or rabbit? She arrives and drops her treasure at my feet – a very old battered shoe. I laugh with relief and Harriet looks dejected. She picks up her prize, shakes it violently to make sure it's really dead and trots ahead of me in disgust, turning every few strides as if to convince me of her hunting prowess. Who had owned the shoe? How had he lost it? How did he get home without it? My mind reflects on his misfortune and into the world of shoes and their significance...

★ ★ ★

I had spent several years trying to stretch a totally inadequate income to feed, clothe and buy shoes for my family of four children – the first three of whom were boisterous boys who actually didn't care what went on their feet unless it was a pair of football boots. There was never any debate over which style or colour of shoe; they just wanted out of the shop as quickly as possible.

I then took my daughter for her first real pair of proper grown-up shoes. She was about three years old and she stood in the shop looking at herself in the full length mirror, staring down at the brown buckle shoes – the cheapest pair in the shop that fitted. Her crestfallen look made me ask what was wrong. Her eyes filled with tears as she looked up at me and said:

"I really wanted red shoes with a strap and a button."

I was instantly transported back to the days of desperately wanting new clothes and knowing that the new clothes my elder sisters had would eventually be mine, and with the absolute longing to have something new that was just mine and not a hand-me-down. It was the same longing I saw in my daughter's eyes then.

Izzie got her new red shoes, with a strap and buttons; they were totally impractical, didn't match anything, looked faintly ridiculous with most outfits, but were very precious to her… and to me. They represented an indulgence, a wasteful expenditure in a world of budgetary constraints that can make us as small-minded as the coins left in our purse. I never regretted that extravagance – a joy for Izzie, a lesson for me – sometimes just go with it, just do it and don't count the cost, however unyielding the budget.

★ ★ ★

We're really stretching our legs this morning, Harriet and I. We've been walking for quite some time and now we've hit the town. It's a bright sunny morning but somehow we've not quite got the timing right so we're just meeting all those who are off to work early. I decide to stop and have a coffee, sitting outside on the pavement. I still feel like a decadent spendthrift when I indulge like this. It remains a luxury that has more to do with taking pleasure in the lack of the morning rush that accompanies retirement than any real need for either rest or rations. The smell of the coffee is enticing. Even Harriet joins in with my mood by lying down and just watching what's going on as the world rolls by. It's as though she's mirroring my feelings of wanting everyone to slow down and enjoy the morning, rather than looking quite so harassed, all hurrying along, worrying what this day will bring, or perhaps how much they've got to get done.

★ ★ ★

I remember how, such a short time ago, I was part of that morning hustle, when there just never felt as though there was time to catch my breath, let alone relax over a coffee. I decide to move on, taking my mug of frothy coffee with me. As we walk on, I become anxious to get away from the beginnings of the morning rush – it feels almost contagious and I certainly don't want to catch it.

This feels a precious time in my life; a special, almost carefree time that I find myself wanting to savour. I never expected that, after leaving work, life would be full of good things and yet be so devoid of the rush exhibited here. I don't think I gave much thought to what retirement might be like. It was as though it was a non-place at the end of something, but almost as though it was something you passed through on your way to somewhere else. I never looked on it as a destination in itself, with something of its own to discover.

We head for home and I begin to think that while I never really considered where the 'somewhere else' was after passing through retirement village, the signpost would surely have to say 'Growing old – this way'.

These thoughts throw an image in front of me, as if on a cinema screen. The picture is of a long line drawn from one side of the display to the other with the title 'Lifeline' above it. It has the years of my life marked on it from left to right. Peaks are being drawn like mountains above the line, indicating good times, with some less impressive, smaller peaks dipping below the line, indicating unhappy times: it's demonstrating a sort of graph design of my life.

2

ALL THE WAY BACK

A really wonderful walk today: not particularly good weather, a bit drizzly and dreary, although Harriet doesn't seem to register the dismal landscape. She's still rushing to and fro, sniffing at everything, running up the bank and then appearing between the bushes farther up the lane. The cloud cover seems dense and low and it feels as though the dimmer switch needs turning up.

Suddenly, in the dim light, I catch sight of a pair of beautiful woodpeckers at the bottom of the meadow, pecking away at the ground, busily unearthing breakfast. I can't hear them but their head movements seem to indicate that they're chatting. First one listening to his partner and then she taking her turn, heads bobbing and tipping, both watching the other, while constantly looking around for signs of danger.

Harriet is way ahead down the lane so there's no chance she'll disturb them and I'm able to stand by the gap in the hedge and watch them discussing their plans for the day. I fancy she's the busy-looking one, forever foraging, while he, with his vivid red head and bright green plumage, stands tall and proud on a mossy stone just above her. It seems she then turns her back on him, dismissing him, indicating it's time for him to get out from under her feet and be off to work. As he lifts from the ground in flight, she casts a backward glance, as if reminding him to return in time for tea: a magic moment in this quite ordinary day, watching as a secret spectator these lovely creatures going about their daily lives.

I'm not quite sure why but my mind runs back to my childhood home and something about the scene I'm witnessing reminds me of my mother who was constantly on the go, always, it seemed, able to do several things at the same time and, as a result, always saying something over her shoulder while her hands were busy.

My mum, Eleanor Latham, was four feet ten inches tall and wore a size four shoe. Her footsteps hold strong memories for me. She always wore very high-heeled shoes, even around the house, and I would lay in bed at night tracing the sound and guessing where she was and what she was doing by the click of those heels – the sound I went to sleep to and the sound I woke up to – my comforter; the function satisfied by a bit of blanket or scruffy teddy bear for my own children in later years.

Even as you looked at her it was evident to all that there was more to my mother than was suggested by her size. Her own mother had died when my mother was just nine years old: my grandfather came home after the First World War to find my grandmother, his thirty-eight-year-old wife, dying with tuberculosis. In quiet moments, perhaps when she was darning socks or clearing out the hearth, if encouraged, Mum would sometimes talk to me in bits and pieces about her life at home.

I think this is where I got the beginnings of what became a deep-rooted fascination for how ordinary folks lived their lives – something that stayed with me as a district nurse – who was at the end of every garden path or at the top of every staircase in the block of flats?

I remember Mum describing how she peered through the brass bedstead rails of her mother's bed on the morning she died. She heard her mother saying she could hear the birds singing. My mum sat on the edge of the bed to hook up her black button boots for school and wondered why she herself couldn't hear the birds that her mother was listening to. Those very same words were spoken by my father in his last moments of consciousness before he died. Mum talked of the shock of returning from school to find her mother had died, of how she wished she had known she was dying so that she could have said goodbye to her. We sat together, for many hours and days, by my father's bed while he was dying, with Mum refusing to leave, even to sleep. She had to be there; she had to say goodbye. As the tears rolled down her face, I felt sure there were tears there for her mother too.

I seldom saw my mother cry but, as I grew up, I had the strong impression that she cried alone. When I was a toddler she would cuddle me on her lap in times of distress and I grew up remembering one of her sayings: 'Don't cry today. Wait till tomorrow.'; the implication being that you needed to save the tears because things might be worse tomorrow. Or maybe, 'Don't let the tears start. Once the floodgates are open, you may never stop.'

Although she always spoke lovingly of her father, he married again, and Mum spoke with coldness about her stepmother, who it seems rejected her, her sister and younger brother. Her stepmother went on to produce a much favoured half-brother and sister. Mum went to work at age fourteen and in the evening played the piano for the silent films at the local cinema in Gerrards Cross – a lucrative addition to her income: a whole shilling (5p) for an evening's playing.

Mum was to repeat this performance for myself and my sisters many times, and again to the delight of my own children. Verbally she gave them the black and white silent film story of the distressed maiden tied to the railway line while she matched her hands to the words. Her gift of playing by ear was a thread that ran through her life and touched all who knew her. From playing 'God Save the King' at the end of some school play, to evenings around her much loved piano singing 'Bless 'em all' and 'Pack up your troubles' with the mildly merry cricket club at the end of a successful match, Mum's piano playing was at the very heart of it all: it fed her soul. Everything she played was slightly syncopated, even when it was a hymn. I heard some Scott Joplin on the radio recently and found myself close to tears. It felt as though she was right there in the next room playing, as I was just coming in the back door, home from school.

I remember sitting on top of this piano in a biscuit-coloured, appliquéd nightdress, aged about four, with my red hair rolled in rags, getting progressively dizzy on home-made elderflower wine. I then fell asleep, curled up like a contented cat, while the singing and jollity went on.

My father came from the next village, from a family who had at one time been quite wealthy. He spent his childhood in Australia, returning to England in his early teens to their home in Chalfont St. Giles. This, the home of my paternal grandparents, seemed very palatial to me as a child. I used to run upstairs to press the bells in each bedroom, slide down the banisters and run across the stone-flagged kitchen floor to see the wobbling room numbers on the wall plaque that had once summoned the servants. To do this was an act of extreme bravery – there was a terrifying monster of a stuffed bird in a glass cabinet at the top of the stairs!

I can imagine this lifestyle captivating my mother, who ran away from her unfriendly stepmother's home on Gold Hill Common to marry the charming, rather roguish character of my father who took her pillion dirt-track riding on his motorcycle. Together they won much local acclaim and many awards for their motorcycle achievements.

My two elder sisters were on the scene when the Second World War was declared and my father, in typical flamboyant style, signed up on the first available day, despite being in a reserved occupation. His exploits as a despatch rider were later to enthral us, including how he was invalided out of the army after Dunkirk. He was listed as 'missing believed killed' for several weeks and landed up in an English hospital, having escaped on one of the last Red Cross boats to leave St. Nazaire.

I arrived, rather unexpectedly I'm told, to take my place in the family; a wartime baby. My childhood meandered happily through the cowslip fields, paddling in the River Misbourne and feeding the ducks on the village pond.

★ ★ ★

I would love to have been able to walk Harriet through a cowslip field. There is a harshness about the golden celandines that inhabit part of one of the walks we're on today. They run along the side of our path as we head downhill to where the field bursts into view when we come out of the wood. Harriet bounds ahead of me here, all the way down to the little brick bridge over the river where I used to bring the children to play Pooh sticks. I lean on the brick edge of the little bridge and Harriet comes and jumps her front paws up next to me, just to see what I'm looking at. I watch the fish as they disappear beneath me and I cross to watch them emerge swimming downriver on the other side of the bridge. The river is very clear with bright green weeds streaking across just beneath the surface of the stream. There are the beginning buds of what looks like a wild water lily beginning to push up through the water as the fish wiggle past. The rounded stones lie undisturbed on the river bed, smoothed by the water's journey.

★ ★ ★

But these gaudy celandines lining our route to the river have neither the charm nor the profusion of those glorious cowslip fields of my childhood – me ankle deep in their nodding heads, returning home with two hands clasped around the stems, presenting Mum with my find and her placing them on the scrubbed kitchen table in the white milk jug.

The village pond in Chalfont St. Giles holds many memories. I sat on its banks the day sweet rationing was abolished with an enormous bag of assorted goodies, unable to believe that the local shopkeeper was not demanding coupons as well as my pocket money. I stood every day on my way to school and threw stones into the pond, watching the ripples spread out carrying my thoughts, joys, frustrations and tears all the way to the bank, while I fed the ducks with my crusts. The crusts were from breakfast, smuggled into my satchel when no-one was looking; at least, if she did know, Mum never let on and allowed me to feel triumphant at my deception. I still hate crusts, but I don't have to feel guilty about leaving them anymore because Harriet devours them as though they are some precious delicacy, allowing me to pretend that actually they are the best bit that I have saved exclusively for her; so the dishonesty, indeed the fraud, continues.

There was a security in that village pond, its constancy: the undulating wrinkles in the water were always there, even when the ducks had wandered off for a walk in the fields. I seemed to gain the same comfort from this scene then, just as I do now from watching waves crashing on the shore, with the monotonous back and forth of the tide.

The coach used to pull up by the pond for the Sunday School outing for us all to clamber aboard, egg and cress sandwiches packed into a creaky Oxo tin in a brown paper carrier bag with string handles. These handles cut into the palms of your hands at the end of the day, when it was heavily laden with shells from the beach and the very damp, hand-knitted swimsuit wrapped in a towel. This yearly event to Hayling Island was dependent upon Sunday School attendance. Each week, a shiny stamp depicting a picture from the church calendar – Septuagesima, Rogation Sunday, the four weeks of Advent – was stuck in the assigned booklet to be surrendered prior to the allocation of seats on the coach. Too many blanks and the coach would draw away, leaving me on the bank of the pond feeding the ducks, bemoaning my fate.

The oak tree on the far side of the pond was privy to my first real passionate kiss. His name was Danny. He had large, dark brown eyes and I still wish I had eyelashes as long as his were. I think I was just sixteen, but I can't be sure. What I remember with certainty was that he thought my freckles were beautiful. It does a girl a really good turn to be told, even if only once in her life, that she's beautiful. We walked home holding hands, with me wondering whether my mother would be able to tell when she looked at me that I had allowed him to undo the top two buttons on my blouse and fondle my breasts. Still there, the oak tree; as are the breasts, though not quite so pert as then, but they, like the oak tree, have experienced the passing of time and yet they still take pleasure in being fondled.

★ ★ ★

We're over here in the fields by the pond, Harriet and I walking along by the River Misbourne where I paddled so often as a child. The fields are verdant with lush grass because of the recent rain. It's a shallow stream and, as Harriet goes in to paddle, it's just up to the tops of her legs. She's struggling to work out how to grab the stick that's under water resting on the stones on the bottom. The refraction caused by the water means she keeps sticking her nose down to where she thinks it is and then can't find it easily because it seems to have moved! Eventually she masters it, flings her head up with stick in mouth and runs about shaking and splashing. She really is not an attractive dog when she's wet; all straggly and bony-looking without her fluffy coat.

I head off away from the stream up towards the footpath and Harriet gallops after me. I go through a gap in the hedge towards the top end of the meadow and as I enter the next door field I realise how much longer the grass is here – at least calf level, probably due to the lack of the presence of any cows here now. Harriet loves to roll around in the long, feathery-topped grass which dries her coat off somewhat and, as we walk on, she becomes her usual ruffled, scruffy self.

Quite suddenly, I stop in my tracks, unable to believe what I'm seeing just ahead of us on the footpath. Emerging from the taller grass on one side, crossing our track and hurrying into the grass on the other side, is a mother duck being followed by her family of ducklings; at least seven or eight of them, still quite young with little brown feathers developing amongst their still yellow fluffy coats. Harriet is as surprised as I am at the display just about six feet in front of us. Before I can stop her, Harriet prances into the middle of the ducklings, carefully stepping over and around them, ears pricked up, with her eyes focused curiously on their quick movements. She makes no attempt to attack them, but mother duck becomes concerned, facing Harriet and quacking loudly. Harriet goes into a play bow that unsettles the mother duck even more. With Harriet refusing to pay any attention to either my voice or whistle calling her to heel, mother duck takes off and flies low just above Harriet's head and lands a bit farther down the slope. When she sees this has no effect on the pesky dog, she repeats the manoeuvre, and repeats it again. I then realise this clever duck is 'performing' to draw Harriet away from her brood… and it works. She takes off, again flying low over the grass, but now she isn't landing, she's flying off. Inevitably, Harriet gives chase, her head and tail becoming visible above the waving grass heads with each bound as she struggles to keep up. She runs and runs until she is only just visible as she disappears through a hedge quite a distance away now.

While I know it's all about the game of chase for Harriet, and that she has no intention of catching the duck, I'm now worried that the ducklings have been abandoned, all because Harriet is just too nosy. I call and whistle and am just beginning to wonder what to do next when I see her appear back through the far hedge, running as fast as she can to get back to me.

Meanwhile, the ducklings seem to have disappeared; no quacky noises, nothing visible anywhere. I then notice a few wavy movements from tall grasses a few feet away in the direction the mother duck had taken. The ducklings have all huddled in together, totally hidden, and there isn't a sound.

Having put Harriet on the lead, I decide to take her away to the top of the field in exactly the opposite direction to that taken by Mrs Duck, and I stoop down behind a clump of blackberry bushes and wait to see what happens. I'm almost holding my breath when minutes later this mother duck comes back, swooping in low a short way from where she was forced to leave her ducklings. She quacks loudly and, almost immediately, I can hear loud chunterings of the ducklings as they head towards the comforting sound of their mother's voice. As I wait, I can just see the grass begin to move as the little party heads down to the river.

I want to stay and watch for longer but I don't trust Harriet not to try to disrupt things again so, reluctantly, I move on. The whole episode hasn't lasted more than ten minutes. How lucky I am to have caught it and to be able to carry with me the magical image of this delightful family outing off for a swim on this glorious morning.

★ ★ ★

Any unfortunate times in my childhood were swept away by the excitement created by an eccentric father who would wake us really early on a sunny morning and announce that we weren't going to school today as we were going to the seaside instead! We crammed into the car and sang and laughed all the way. By the time we reached Stoke Poges on the outward journey, my father's voice would ring out:

"The next person who says 'are we nearly there yet' gets no ice cream today."

Mum would then pass a large bag of freshly picked peas on to our laps in the back of the car and we would spend the rest of the journey popping the pods and eating the peas. The busy hands made for a quieter journey.

That little old standard eight seems to have gone right through my childhood, becoming progressively more dilapidated. That old jalopy would frequently break down on these unauthorised trips, and we either filled the radiator from puddles with our flask cups or held the fabric roof on as we bumped home. The whole journey was punctuated with somebody returning from behind a hedge in various stages of undress with cow parsley protruding beneath a skirt hem, held fast by an elasticated knicker leg.

I remember always being worried that we would get lost and not be able to find our way home. I still struggle not to panic when I can't find my way… a frequent occurrence exacerbated by a total lack of any sense of direction, combined with a total inability to read a map.

Mum went quietly about her duties throughout it all, making sure Dad was comfortable. Much of my mother's time and energy seemed to be about ensuring my father's comfort. I remember watching her as she put the sugar in his tea, the cup sitting in the palm of his big steady hand, his other hand resting on his knee, while she stirred. I suppose we girls all grew up learning that men were to be waited on and that, as wives, it was supposed to be our mission in life to serve our men.

Our home had an easy feel that resembled a patchwork quilt: nothing matched anything but it had a homely, lived-in feel about it; an ambiance I think I have copied now in my own small resting place. I like the chaotic warmth I learned from that home setting.

I was surprised to find that after I divorced and moved to my much smaller house, my choices in furnishings and colours were very different from those I'd lived with while married. As I look back, I think I took very little part in choosing things then. Now I've discovered I prefer a somewhat jumbled décor that looks 'lived in' rather than the regimented, very tidy one I had become used to in my married years. I find I've got pictures up of mine that were previously put away because they weren't somehow approved of. I really like them even though the colours don't actually match the interior decoration.

My childhood home was an appropriate backcloth for Dad's traditional jazz music, and many evenings resounded with loud jazz rhythm; my dad on the guitar and Mum, of course, on the piano. I can still recall my father's black and white 'correspondent' shoes that he wore when his band was off on a booking at some village hall. We should have had a jazz band at your funeral, Dad; you'd have liked that!

My mother suffered badly when all her daughters left home, which we did more or less together – my eldest sister got married, my middle sister entered the police force and I went into a nursing career in London at Charing Cross Hospital in the Strand. The gentle goodness and strength she had given us so consistently meant that she had developed her happiness around us and had pursued very few interests of her own. Her life focused almost entirely on Dad; his wants, his needs, and his requests. As his demands multiplied, her servitude intensified, permitting further pleas from him for more attention. By the time he died, he was quite a tyrant and my mother somewhat downtrodden.

3

FAMILY DYNAMICS

We walked home this morning across 'Harriet's garden', the triangular patch over the road that passes our front door. It's a much bigger piece of ground than the usual triangle in the middle of three roads. This one is probably about half an acre in size. It is glowing with the yellow buttercups dancing on their long stems. The grass around them bordering the woodland copse is lush, while further in, under the trees, some bluebells are just finishing; their brightest blue colouring has faded and the flower heads are over blown. They are scattered in clumps with the wild ramsons, with their garlic scent seeming to have bedded in around them.

The war memorial embellishes the corner nearest home. I try to make sure Harriet gives it a wide berth, discouraging her from sniffing too enthusiastically around the stone base. It somehow feels disrespectful to allow her to trample around in front of the engraved names; no poppy wreaths there just now but it's still a place of reverence, a state of deference never practised by Harriet.

I pick a few buttercups and put them in a thin tall vase. Their stems stand straight and lofty with the delicate gold flowers accentuated against the clutter of books on my dresser behind them.

★ ★ ★

The good memories were still happening over the years: walking again over those meadows with Mum and my own children, her grandchildren; watching my auburn-haired toddler's delight as she plunged her fingers into my mother's button bag, letting the brightly coloured buttons cascade from her hands. I could physically feel the pleasure I had felt doing the same thing as a child. We walked through the bluebell-carpeted woods that were always in bloom for my mother's birthday, with my children picking Nana a bunch to take home. I don't think I'll ever stand in such a wood again, with the bright green beech leaves overhead and the dense blue blooms beneath my feet, without an uncontrollable yearning for my mother – to have her by my side again, to hear her laugh, to smell her 'Bluegrass' cologne.

I've asked my own children to scatter my ashes in a bluebell wood when my time comes.

My mother grieved terribly for my middle sister, who moved away at about the time I got married and deliberately never contacted my mother again; no row, no great reason, she simply refused to respond to my mother's longing to see her. It was a huge cruelty. Right up to the day she died, my mother's heart ached just to hear from her, ached for her return, never understanding what she had done or why she had been so forsaken by her. Mum always felt guilty, saying she thought my sister was paying her back for when she had left her in the hospital aged three years old. She'd been quite ill and in those days parents weren't allowed to do more than look through the oval window in the ward door at visiting times. Mum felt that my sister had always been determined to return what she perceived to be this abandonment by her.

I remember from time to time, maybe it was on particular dates, birthdays and suchlike, Mum would put fresh flowers in my sister's bedroom with a note saying 'Love can wait'.

I'm not sure I have any explanation as to why, but I made almost no effort to intervene, to contact her, to try and repair the relationship between my sister and my mum or to maintain any relationship with her myself. I saw her on very few occasions, I think twice, and when I attempted to talk about how much Mum wanted to see her she said that she'd never really liked her, didn't want to see her and had no intention of doing so. I suppose I knew she wouldn't. She had never been willing to do anything she didn't want to, ever, so I think I accepted then that she wasn't going to change now. She had always behaved as though all members of our family were less than she deserved, as though it was a huge wrong that had been visited upon her to be born into our family. Many years later we learned that she revelled in telling stories about how the family had disowned her. Maybe it was that untruth, that duplicity, that led me to do nothing more. I have always found both deliberate cruelty and lies intolerable ways of making or fostering relationships; when those two attributes become bedfellows they are a force for evil that scares me. Maybe it was fear that held me back. She had always been a powerful force within the family; perhaps, despite my mother's longing, I was relieved when she left.

An added sadness for my mother was that she was so pleased to have had three girls, often saying how wonderful it was because we would always have each other after she and Dad had gone. In fact, we were none of us able to forge really close relationships with each other. I don't think at any point in our lives could we have been described as close sisters. I remember saying this to a cousin once and he confirmed my thoughts, commenting that of course it could never be so; that he knew no other family where sisters were all so very different with such disparate personalities and aims in life and that it would be impossible for any of us to ever be close friends.

My eldest sister and I accepted our differences. I'm not sure we ever really understood each other but we cared about each other, we lived close and always remained in contact. We looked at life very differently but were able to allow one another to be the way we were without malice or forethought, just knowing what we wanted from life was fundamentally different but always accepting that as okay. I sometimes think that maybe we would have learned to understand each other better in my retirement years, had she lived longer. Maybe we would have shared some walks with Harriet. Neither of us believed that a deeper understanding with my middle sister was a possibility, or even something we wanted to contemplate; neither of us made any meaningful attempt to make it happen.

It occurs to me now, only as I labour to articulate my feelings surrounding these family dynamics, just how much of my working life was spent, at very intimate life stages, with so many varied relative groupings; having, and enabling, difficult conversations between close family members at very stressful times. Also, how often I was able to battle on a patient's behalf for what he or she needed or wanted and yet I failed to step up and even try to accomplish what my mother wanted – to have her other daughter visit her.

In my professional life I became known for managing these complex, demanding interactions with families competently – moving families through stages of mutual pretence; a situation with each side keeping up a front for the other that all would be well. This pretence was so often played out by partners, each pretending that things were getting better when each knew, but was unable to share, that there would be no holiday together next year despite the deception of planning for it. Breaking down these barriers often enabled precious last weeks and months of someone's life to be spent close to their loved ones, rather than both parties struggling with the loneliness that develops from the massive distance that grows when everyone, including the health professionals, play the game of 'don't let's talk about it'.

Did I go on to make happen in my career what I had been so incapable of performing at home?

It has to be that we learn what we live. I think I learned about 'waiting for love' from my mother. I learned to serve the man I married, somehow believing I had to earn the right to be loved. As the years went on, the denigration of me increased while I struggled to 'do better' and to 'wait for the love' that would surely follow if I could prove I was good enough.

I never filled the gap my missing sister left in my mother's life but, as I grew older, we seemed to share a companionship that I cherished. I was, for much of this time, very unhappy in my own marriage, bewildered and frightened, yet with a dogged determination to make it work that must have come from my mother.

★ ★ ★

Harriet seems to be enjoying this morning's autumnal walk as much as I am. It's glorious: the colours magnificent, the row of trees tracking down Rectory Hill have changed colour, forming their own private spectacular rainbow, ranging from bright yellow through gold, all the reds and russets ending with the browns. Autumn: so beautiful, yet so fleeting, somehow emphasising the bitter sweetness of it.

★ ★ ★

Dad died and my marriage disintegrated around me. That autumn, the falling leaves seemed to take on a new meaning as I scrunched them beneath my feet. It was my favourite season of the year but now it seemed to symbolise my life tumbling about me and I no longer felt strong enough to hold on through it. With its harsh, cold winds, one by one my dreams were tugged off my tree and lay scattered around me on the ground… they were trampled into the mud as I fought to rescue some remnants of anything. I felt buried under them, in danger of also being trodden into the mire.

As autumn expired so did my marriage. There was a desperate need for me to pull the threads of life together again; to make life happen once more for my beautiful, innocent children.

Mum ached for me as mothers do. This frail little lady was

there for me again, although I dared not lean on her. Her support for me was absolute: no judging, no criticism. She began to put her own life together without my father as I began to rebuild mine, and we shared glasses of her favourite dry sherry and precious talks in her new diminutive ground floor flat near me.

But it was really all too late for her. There wasn't enough of her candle left to burn brightly anymore; it fluttered and flickered frequently with ill-health and, at times, became very dim and in danger of being snuffed out by the latest bout of pleurisy or pneumonia. Each took hold more quickly and every time recovery took longer.

There was the night she was dying, when she asked me to leave her at home and not send her into hospital again. She had laid out all her documents, pension book, deeds to the flat... I climbed into her single bed with her, cradled her in my arms and waited for her to die. As the first morning light came I could see that the pneumonia wasn't allowing her to slip away as peacefully as she wanted. She was now in heart failure, restless and gasping. I decided to transfer her to hospital in the hope of some sedation rather than allow her to struggle to an unpleasant end. You should have died that night Mum, it was what you wanted and I would have felt I'd done the right thing by you... being there when your candle went out.

After several weeks she came home but was unable to rally to full health and strength again. She needed more care from me than she found acceptable and she was impatient with my interference. The loss of independence was intolerable for her and she fought me at every turn. This tiny being, defiant to the end, tossed her head in the air and refused to accept that maybe she needed help. She could never adjust to the changing role of me looking after her instead of her looking after me. Bloody hell, life is cruel to the elderly: they teach us everything we know and then we turn round and tell them we know best. I tried hard to get it right, but I don't think I made it.

We had a lovely Christmas: my eldest sister was a wonderful cook and Mum had her seven grandchildren and two of her daughters around her. She carved the turkey as she'd always done and partook in a frail way in the jollities. My eldest son, Mum's grandson, took great delight in furtively sneaking her favourite whisky tipple to her on the quiet behind my back. She became quite tipsy while I played the game and pretended not to notice as they shared the conspiracy together like two naughty children.

There was a sudden cold snap early that following January. Snow fell fast over the first weekend of the New Year of 1983. I took her meals and settled her in the warm. On Sunday morning I had a phone call from the hospital to say she had collapsed in the snow, out on her own, and was 'dead on arrival' at the hospital... would I please go and identify the body.

Eleanor Latham; you once again left home against advice... this time to die. Did you have to take your right to independence that far, Mum? Maybe it was the last decision you could make for yourself. Perhaps it was right for you.

The open grief I felt at her death felt too deep to ever recover from. Even now, so many years later, there are times when I struggle to pull my feet free from the mire of memory so that I'm able to see the clear sky above.

I have a picture in my mind of Mum standing in front of her full length mirror, in her outrageously high heels, feet apart, hands in pockets at the beginning of the day, holding her head high, with a determined air, just about to 'gird her loins' for another day.

4

WHAT NEXT?

Within just over a year, both Mum and Dad had died and my husband had left. It felt as though anyone who'd ever cared for me had disappeared out of my life. I felt enveloped in an unresolved litany of grief from which I couldn't escape.

★ ★ ★

A sudden gust crept through a cluster of trees at an exposed corner on the edge of the big wood and caught both of us unawares. Harriet's shaggy coat flew in all directions as the wind caught it and as she pounced on the crisp golden leaves as they danced. The threat of winter hung in the grey sky but it was as though autumn was trying to hang on to her mellow fruitfulness for just a little longer. It was a lovely season that leant itself to reminiscence; we had been out far too long, it had been a long walk and my thoughts had meandered even farther than our feet… but then Harriet did have four and I have only two. I guess my memories extended over more years than hers and, therefore, while she had managed to keep focused, nose to the ground, my head had gone on a separate journey to my feet. We were quite a way from home as my head and feet connected. There was a decided chill in the air; I turned up my collar and quickened my step. She seemed to sense my deliberation, along with my bitter-sweet recollections, and came to heel, coming so close she brushed my leg with each step as if to remind me that I was still loved and needed.

★ ★ ★

Mum's dying taught me that love doesn't die at death; there is a space between those last happenings and definitive death. Somewhere in the silence of that intermission, the relationship changes, the dimension relocates, it modifies, but it does continue; its strength lives on. I never had any experience of her after she died; no hallucination like those of many after losing a loved one, nothing that substantial, nothing so easily explained. But there was a strengthened feeling of certainty about life following its predestined pattern. While she was now on the right side of the tapestry and clearly able to see the pattern, I was still working with the rich colours on the reverse of the work, weaving all the threads into position. We're working together on the same piece of work: all we have shared, all we have experienced, laughed about, talked about; the love we have shared goes on. It is all part of the same journey, death being part of that journey. Nothing that ever happened between us, nothing we ever said to one another is lost – it's still here, it still lives on.

Not so a broken marriage. This man I had loved, trusted and believed in for more than twenty years seemed to have neither the principles nor the integrity I had supposed. He was able to absent himself from mine and the children's lives without a backward glance it seemed; to write us all off as though we had never existed. What did that say of my judgement of character? To be so mistaken meant all certainty gone, all sands shifting, leaving me pulled down into the quicksand, threatening my every breath. How was I ever to trust my way of thinking when it had let me down so badly?

It was at this time that I began sifting in my mind the variations between grieving when a partner leaves to go on to another life, and grieving when losing a partner to death. After death he may indeed be travelling to another life, but one we won't actually get to know the details of. While there are many parallels between these losses, there are also distinct differences. When you lose a partner to death, you don't lose his love. When your partner chooses to leave you, you are left with the reality that he took away the love he had once given you, to give to someone else. I found this shook my belief system, made me doubt myself and lose confidence in my own thought processes.

It was many months, probably a couple of years, before I could enjoy looking at the family photograph albums again. Previously, I would look at a picture of a family day out with us all having a picnic and I would think, 'I believed that was a happy day'. He says he was always unhappy in the relationship and never enjoyed such times. How could I have read it so wrongly? How do I trust what I believe to be true ever again?

Nothing Left

The girl who once lived here has gone away,
The girl who adored you has fled.
She who wove round you a carpet of dreams,
While you slept in another girl's bed.
She stood on the shore and she waited,
Worn by the wind and the rain.
Worn by the sky and the rocks and the sand:
She waited and waited again.
At last in the cold grey of morning,
She picked up her pumice stone heart;
The dance of the sunlight had faded,
The magic had fallen apart.
Gone were the gold and the yellow;
Gone were the pink and the red;
The colours she treasured had trickled away,
While you slept in another girl's bed.

Sadness seemed to become the skin I lived in for a while; so many losses, stirred continually by changes: returning to full-time work, moving house, great financial insecurities. I remember an almost burning need to find my sense of humour again, running alongside fear, fear that it had perished – that there would never be a return to times when, with absolutely everything going wrong, impromptu laughter would make everything seem all right again. Children learn what they live. I wanted fun back in their lives.

★ ★ ★

Harriet suddenly bounded ahead and turned to face me with jaws clamped on a stick. She immediately went into play bow mode, with front paws splayed wide and hind quarters up in the air, topped by a vigorously wagging tail. She is an expert in absurdity. She understands the real meaning of fun.

★ ★ ★

One day, hurt gave way to hope; humour reached into the dark pit and showed me a way forward, offering me healing.

A letter to the mistress from the wife

Now that my husband has decided to leave and move in with you after the rather clandestine affair that I gather has swept you both off your feet, I thought you might find his transition from lover to live-in partner somewhat difficult to cope with.

A few helpful hints gathered over the last twenty years might be useful.

He likes his toilet things kept separately on his side of the bathroom cabinet, not all jumbled up with yours – please note this is very important.

Don't worry too much about his lack of communication in the mornings; it's nothing to do with you, it's something to do with his body clock and unfortunately it's getting worse as he gets older. Emergence from nocturnal slumbers is often accompanied by a headache. Hot sweet tea, cold flannels on the forehead, crushed codeine and effervescent salts seems to do the trick on most occasions. Failure to provide these can cause the mood to move rapidly through the irritability zone to sheer bad temper, which can quite ruin a weekend, so it's advisable to check stocks of same regularly!

It's a good idea to make sure the hall table is clear for him to put his briefcase on when he comes in from work. It gets the evening off to a really bad start if he has to put it on the floor.

While we're on the subject of the hall table, it's advisable to dust it, however hastily, when you hear his key in the door, as any hint of finger marks seems to indicate that you have lain on the sofa all day popping chocolate mints in your mouth – a squirt of spray polish in the air before he opens the door works wonders. Incidentally, a bottle of wine served with a rushed supper will sometimes stave off the comments about the frozen meal too.

I'll enclose his foot cream with the rest of his things. He likes to apply it at night, sitting on the edge of the bed last thing. I've tried for many years to persuade him to do it in the bathroom with no success, I'm afraid. The toenail picking that accompanies this can be a bit of a turn-off, particularly if you've donned the black negligee and planned a night of bodice-ripping passion! It's probably better to stay in the perfumed bath a little longer and try to time your entrance into the bedroom between the foot creaming ceremony and when he falls asleep… can be tricky!

By the way, the bottom sheet will always be smoothed, however carefully you've made the bed, and the pillow will be turned twice before it's fit to lie on.

Of course, I don't need to tell you not to be quite so trusting as I was, and maybe you need to be a bit suspicious about those meetings at work that go on rather late. I believed him always; maybe you shouldn't.

Take care of him, hug him, cherish him, and I hope you can love him for as long as I have. Be patient with him, don't ask him to push away his past too quickly. No, he wasn't married to someone who didn't understand him; it was a marriage full of love and laughter before you came on the scene. He finds it difficult to talk about feelings but there are bound to be times when he reflects and wonders where twenty years of life with me and his four beautiful children has gone.

I guess it's difficult to build a relationship on lies, deceit and other people's unhappiness. I hope you succeed, for both your sakes.

From the wife

P.S. He likes the crusts cut off his sandwiches and same cut
in half lengthways.

I wrote this letter on the day I 'celebrated' my decree absolute. As
I re-read it now, some twenty-five plus years after it was scripted,
the pain is there on the page; without my diary I wouldn't be able
to recall its intensity.

It took time to get over the emotional bruising but healing
happens; something lifts the misery and I began to discover that I
was happy again. It was to take me some long time before I
recognised how good it was to live my own life, rather than always
struggling to avoid his displeasure. Needing to work harder than
I'd ever imagined for many years to maintain the family was as
nothing compared with that struggle.

When I turned out my mother's flat after her funeral I found a
roll of my school reports tied up in a green ribbon in the bottom of
her ottoman. I sank to my knees on the floor with anticipation,
excited to read them. My eyes filled with tears as I found the same
or similar comments repeated throughout all of them.

'Dinah has worked extremely hard this term. C-'

I seemed to have spent most of my schooldays continually
striving, always working hard, to accomplish very little. Had my
life been a continual battle to repeatedly fail?

It actually took another forty years for me to be able to finally
realise that maybe the failure labels that had haunted me weren't
altogether accurate. I was fifty years old when I used my annual leave
allowance to attend university one day a week to achieve my master's
degree, while still working full-time as a district nurse. I then began
to lecture in both palliative and community nursing. I still don't
know whether 'late developer' or 'slow learner' is the pertinent term
for me; perhaps both. But what I do know is that to write someone
off as academically unable at the age of eleven is absurd.

5

THE CAREER BEGINS

It's a most glorious walk this morning. The cow parsley is piled high on either side of the footpath, like two big frothy waves threatening to collapse and crash down and meet one another. I stride forward like Moses commanding the sea to part before me, while Harriet's tail wags high, joining the white flower waves, first this side and then that.

We walk on along the bridle path that has the main wood on the right and a line of large trees to the left; they are unusual trees, with much of their root formation above ground. Harriet has a great time jumping up and over them, and weaving in and out and down the mossy bank to run up again and round the next one. It's quite a dark wood most of the day and, somehow, the rooted trees seem quite foreboding. I'm glad when we veer right and head up the steep hill into the back of the crescent where, although it's still quite early, there are signs of life.

There are a couple of suited and booted gentlemen with their briefcases hurrying off to the station, and a newspaper delivery lad throws his bike up against the hedge and runs up the path, hastily pushing the paper through the letterbox, a resounding clatter announcing its arrival on the mat the other side. His bike has a wire basket on the front, with both newspapers and a satchel in it. The satchel is bursting open and books are spilling out at the side, all ready to take on to school.

★ ★ ★

I wonder which books they are. I tip my head sideways trying to read a title. What are they about?

I've developed a fondness for my books since I've retired; proper books, not medical textbooks, which is all I seem to have read for years. I'm an incredibly slow reader. Even I can't believe how long it takes me to read a chapter. All through my nursing, particularly in my later post-graduate studies, I spent hour upon hour reading all the necessary research books and papers. Even reading my own essays as I composed them was so time-consuming. There was never time to even read a magazine, let alone some of the wonderful books that now form part of my post-retirement collection. I've spent many a wet weekend absorbed in a book, totally consumed by how many books I still have to discover and read when I am so behind in the race. I don't have enough time or years left to get them all read. I've discovered that non-fiction is my addiction – probably a continuation of my fascination with how people and families live and operate; an extension of the many intimate conversations I had with patients and their families over the years, exchanges which were the heart of the work I did. It's only possible to provide the care people really need if you find out who they are, how the family group functions and what's important to them. To recognise and respond in any significant way to those needs requires setting aside judgements and being prepared to get involved in differences.

I remember reading once (it was Schon's work) that nurses divided roughly into two groups: those who worked on 'the high hard ground' being technically rational and really efficient with equipment; and those who worked in 'the swampy lowlands' where difficult conversations with patients and families were the heart of their craft. I was definitely a 'swampy lowlands' labourer.

A warm walk this morning; a bit of a heat wave, so Harriet and I have left early, done a long walk, using as much woodland as possible to keep us in the shade as the temperature begins to rise. It's not yet nine o'clock but very warm, and even though I have the flimsiest of cotton trousers on, I'm aware that I'd be more comfortable without my gilet. I haven't yet discovered how you dog walk without some article of clothing that will take the mobile phone, door keys, treats, poo bags and, of course when walking with Harriet, the obligatory ball and telescopic thrower.

Harriet, too, is hot and heads for the pond on the north road edge of our common. Normally she delicately dips her head in from the edge and laps, but not today; because it has dried out a bit there is less water and more mud and she heads straight for the tall rushes and plunges in up to her armpits. She gallops out with mud right up to the top of each of her legs. I giggle as she prances along in front of me with these thick black stockings on.

★ ★ ★

The vision of black stockings inevitably throws me back in thought to nurse training and, in particular, I can clearly see all of us in front of me now, as we were the day we got our final exam results. We all sat as a group on the floor of the nurses' lounge at the hospital, shoes off, our black-stockinged legs protruding in all directions beneath our uniforms, some knees curled to the side, some with feet planted firmly, knees being hugged by arms, some long outstretched legs crossed at the ankle – oh, how I wanted those long, long legs with those oh so slim ankles – all sharing the opening of the dreaded results.

It was a day that would be remembered by the whole world forever. Amazingly, *not* because I had become a state registered nurse but because the news broke that President Kennedy had been shot.

We had somehow completed our training and we had passed our finals; a bit of a shock to many of us. According to the Sister Tutor, we were all doomed to fail – the worst 'set' she had ever had to try and turn into professional nurses!

Charing Cross Hospital in the Strand had been our home together and we were about to leave. This grand, old, imposing building with all its tradition had grown on us. It had filled our lives throughout our training. She had been the backcloth to our transformation from wide-eyed student nurses, intent on saving lives and laying hands on fevered brows, to fully qualified, state registered nurses who had grown up fast with the experiences of caring; who worked, for the most part, longer hours than our fathers, who had shared our lives and exhaustion so intimately, many of us bound together with a profound friendship that tied us closer than many a family member. Blood is thicker than water they say. This blood of human experience – of being close to birth and death, to sorrow and gladness, the fears, tears and laughter – was to fasten some of us together throughout our future lives, through all our triumphs and traumas.

That laughter was sometimes very inappropriate hilarity, but was oh so needed. Such as the first day I was allowed on to a ward with actual patients after completing my time in training school with dummies (or classmates) to practise on. Here I was 'let loose' on a ward full of patients, many of whom were elderly. The staff nurse immediately put me to work, instructing me first to clean the sluice room and then to clean all the elderly patients' false teeth. The eagerness with which I undertook this task led me to collect all the pairs of false teeth in the ward into a shiny steel bowl and stride to the sluice to give them the best clean they'd ever had, all twenty or so pairs of them. Unfortunately, I took no account of how I was going to match teeth to patient when I had finished. I was diligently scrubbing before I realised my faux pas and, deep in the pit of my stomach, a sense of panic began to rise and render me incapable of rational thought; an experience that was to be oft repeated throughout my training. I crept round the ward a bed at a time offering up my bowl, "Do you recognise any of these?" I stuttered, each patient staring into my collection of sparkling pearlies. "These look a bit like mine, nurse. Shall I try them for size?" I feel sure some patients were discharged home with a different set of teeth than when they were admitted… and not one of them told Sister.

I owe a huge debt of gratitude to the many patients on numerous occasions who protected me from Sister's wrath, who covered for me and who made sure the eighteen inches of top sheet, that *must* be displayed over the counterpane before Matron's round, was never spoiled with newspaper print.

Sister had an uncanny ability to always be within striking distance whenever some seemingly unforgivable, but probably minor, misdemeanour had occurred and indeed her voice really did 'strike'. "NURSE! Why is this patient in a wet bed?" boomed out across the ward as I was scurrying back to Harry's bed with a clean sheet under my arm. I had spilt the blanket bath water and was rapidly trying to recover the situation before being found out. I slid to a standstill at Sister's feet. My throat tightened as her glare rendered me unable to move. My jaw locked half open.

"It was my fault, Sister. I couldn't wait for the bottle." Harry's voice rang out clear and steady. This gravely ill man suffered the humiliation of allowing Sister to think he'd wet the bed to save me a dressing down for my carelessness.

The laughter was often an expression of exhaustion that so easily tipped over to tears. The linen cupboard bore witness to many an emotional outburst caused by the angst of caring yes, but many times the red eyes that were visible as we surfaced were the result of Sister's wrath. It was to be many years later, when I became a ward Sister myself, that I understood the need for both the discipline and the high standards she demanded, and that driving us so hard was about the insistence of excellence for her patients, not just a cantankerous disposition.

Working such long hours meant that life was reduced to a series of small pleasures: the chance to grab a few minutes illegitimate sleep on a stretcher at 2am, closing your eyes while walking along a corridor, a starched collar that has 'given' enough to stop chafing your neck; finding your black lace-up duty shoes have been unexpectedly polished by a goodly friend. These things take on a sweetness that can't be measured. Sometimes these gifts reached dizzy heights; such as the day another nurse friend and I, both on a split duty (a three-hour afternoon break while working a twelve-hour day), decided to go and see the latest big hit film in Leicester Square. We were in our outdoor uniform queuing to buy tickets when we were called out of line by the manager and escorted to the best seats in the house free of charge – a clear indication of the high esteem in which nurses were held back then.

It was a time when very few women would venture alone at night through the streets of Soho, a stone's throw from the hospital. Yet, in our uniform, we could come and go through any of the back streets with no concern at all. Covent Garden market also ran very close to the hospital and, coming off night duty early in the morning, any bag or basket we were carrying was always filled with fruit and veg as the traders would call a cheery 'G'night nurse'.

All that had gone alongside all the caring and giving that had resounded throughout these old walls, and had got us all through those final exams and brought us to this point.

Here we all were, lined up against the wall, crisp white aprons, starched butterfly caps being hastily adjusted as we donned our capes and filed into Matron's office, one at a time. Here we were told how lucky we were to have had our training here, reminded that we were about to take our places in a profession where we would faithfully serve as those who had gone before us had served and, finally, we were cautioned about the hospital reputation resting on our shoulders.

We were then invited to announce where we now intended to take our nursing career and where our first job as a qualified nurse away from our training hospital was to be. We each took our turn, standing nervously before 'she who must be obeyed', waiting for approval.

There were only two of us who were intending to work on the community from my set of twenty student nurses. The community was always the poor relation of the nursing profession; being seen as less important, less exciting than hospital work where new treatments and interventions were born and the pace was ever-increasing.

Mandy came out from her 'exit interview' looking pale and announcing that Matron had said it was a waste of a good nurse for her to consider nursing on the district; she should not squander her training and should rethink her decision.

It was therefore with some trepidation that I checked the seams in my black stockings, entered through the heavy oak door and strode nervously forward towards the desk, with Matron sitting reverently behind it. The formalities over, I stammered out my desire to work on the community, in patients' homes. She then calmly announced that she believed that this was an ideal choice for the lack of talent I had displayed throughout my training and that nursing was becoming a highly technical profession, for which I had demonstrated little promise. She added that my insistence on carrying out procedures with my left hand, rather than adapting to the correct way of undertaking tasks, had contributed to making my actions appear clumsy and untidy. District nurses just needed to care for people in unsanitary conditions, mainly elderly patients living or dying with chronic diseases, but there would be no call for anything like the nursing expertise I had been trained for… she said.

There was a sense in which she was to be proved right. I needed to learn new skills that I didn't yet know I would need. It takes a different expertise to gain entry to someone's home, when they may be suspicious about what you're about to do, and even greater communication skills to 'fit in' when you're in there. We were still in the days of the patient in hospital accepting what was best for him and being terrified to disobey the hospital rules. The patient in his own home feels more secure and therefore more able to exert his own will and needs. Understanding, tact and persuasion were needed to convince him to accept help, heed advice or comply with treatment.

I was also to discover that 'fitting in' was a new skill I had to learn that was never included in our hospital training syllabus: how to drink tea from a tin mug laced with 'summut to keep cold 'art nurse' (and still be able to stay upright on the bike afterwards); how to hold on to your stomach contents when maggots appeared as you lifted a pendulous abdomen to wash beneath the numerous folds of skin. The owner had been unable to raise her own bulky belly for many months and was now unable to manage her own personal care at all. Equally, I learned how to accept any hospitality offered. If arriving for a visit when high tea was being served, a chair would be pulled out and a nod of the head would demand that I sit and join in. I considered I'd really made it the day I learned to eat egg on toast with no knife or fork at the same time as balancing a two-year-old with a sodden nappy on my lap, while diagnosing a head lice infestation in at least three of the other children.

I was to reflect on the way I was received and welcomed as a district nurse in this London borough when, some twenty or so years later, I moved to work in what would be termed a financially secure area in the south east. Time had marched on and this was a different clientele of upwardly mobile commuting families who would complain if your visit was inconveniently timed. It was here where, on one occasion never to be forgotten, I was requested at my first visit to please use the tradesman's entrance in future rather than the front door! Clearly, new ways of 'fitting in' had to be considered.

But all this lay far ahead. For now all I knew was that I had got through this, the beginning of my career training, even though while I considered I had 'passed' my finals, Matron clearly saw me as a 'failure'; just as my school had seen me as a failure. Indeed I was in their eyes: I failed the dreaded eleven plus which meant I had no brain and would need to be employed using my hands. Hairdressing was promised as I remember. I was becoming used to managing myself as a failure as I sailed forth to my community career.

Anyway, I knew *all* my patients wouldn't be elderly because I was about to do my full midwifery qualification to become a district nurse and midwife, with homebirths and those elderly frail all as part of my caseload; probably in the wilds of Cornwall with a dog on the back seat of my car.

Following my midwifery training at Queen Charlotte's Maternity Hospital – I was now a proud State Certified Midwife – I continued in London to undertake my Queen's District Nurse training; the last leg of my journey to become a district nurse and midwife.

★ ★ ★

Now I want to keep walking to try and get some of the black mud on Harriet's legs to dry and, hopefully, drop off a bit before we reach home when it will discard itself on to my carpet. A field of long grass might help and I'm remembering a suitable one not too far away. I turn off to circle round to find it. Being somewhat geographically challenged, it's impossible for me to know which way I'm heading on any unfamiliar route. I'm concentrating, trying to make sure I'm at least walking in the right direction, towards the field rather than away from it. It's then that I remember just what a disadvantage it was, when I began my district training in London, not to be able to read a map, and how difficult it was for me to learn the layout of the labyrinth of back streets. Maps had always proved fairly useless, with me constantly shuffling them round in my hands trying to decide which way up they should be and if I was at this point, was I facing this way or over that way?

★ ★ ★

The heavy oak desk seemed too big for the short, squat frame of the Sister who interviewed me for my Queen's training. She constantly pushed her glasses up on her nose while her more than ample bosoms polished the green leather surface hidden beneath each one.

Questions seemed to come thick and fast. She hadn't got time to waste, she told me. When could I start? Did I have any pecuniary embarrassments? I mumbled no, wondering what on earth they were and doubting my ability to undertake this job if I didn't even know some of the diseases I might catch.

She first handed me a very well used road map with an area enclosed in a thick blue crayon line, telling me that my area would be Portobello Road and I wasn't to forget that my caseload also included the market stall traders. I folded the map and slipped it into my pocket knowing I would need to study it at length before starting work tomorrow. She hustled me downstairs, flung open the basement door and gesticulated towards the yard, saying that I would need to collect my bike from here and to make sure I wasn't late; there was a lot to do. She then presented me with my Gladstone bag, complete with instruments and my second white bag lining.

I was to learn fast that the instruments had to be boiled up each night and a newly laundered bag lining was to be buttoned into the leather bag weekly. There were strict rules about what was to be carried in these equipment bags and they would be checked randomly by this same Sister who would just announce one morning that she would accompany you on your rounds that day. Woe betide you if she discovered your packet of cigarettes hidden in there! In fact, I learned there was a special bag kept just for this inspection occurrence. Whoever was chosen for the sudden "I'm doing your rounds with you today" would lift this pre-prepared bag as she filed through the 'ops' room to collect her bike. Meanwhile, other nurses would go rapidly ahead to warn all the patients on your round to please have the newspaper laid out on the floor to receive the Gladstone bag, with a further sheet on the chair for the nurse to put her folded coat on, to please borrow the required large tin jug for the hot water from next door (no pouring hot water directly from the kettle into the bowl for the nurse to wash her hands!), to be on their best behaviour, and definitely not to offer the daily cuppa: "Your nurse is being inspected today."

And they always rose to the occasion: everything beautifully laid out, the baked biscuit tin resting in the oven full of cooked, sterile, gauze dressing swabs, the fish paste jar with the thermometer in it and the saucepan on the stove ready boiling to receive the instruments for sterilisation. Bless them; each and every one. On my inspection day even old Mr B managed unusually to keep his hands to himself and didn't take a large pinch of my backside as I passed the bed. Nowadays, he'd be threatened with a sexual harassment suit. Then, the water for the blanket bath would be barely tepid.

When I began my district nursing work in Notting Hill, I was allocated a bike to do my daily rounds. It had a wicker basket, a clanking mudguard and a chain that fell off with monotonous regularity. It never became my friend in all my days on and around Portobello Road, the centre of my patch. It wasn't the trendy smart area it has now become. It was a poor neighbourhood in the '60s but it was always vibrant and colourful. I grew to love it all, and to feel very cared for by all its inhabitants. It was a hardworking, happy time in my career. Many of the stall owners knew me well and often I'd come out after a visit to find, once again, my bicycle basket filled with fruit or vegetables, and on one occasion a huge bunch of flowers with a note saying 'Thanks very much for being so good to my dad.' I never knew who they were from or who the dad was they referred to.

Yes. That bike should have been a beloved companion. But it wasn't.

6

CHILDBIRTH AND MOTHERHOOD

We are doing the big field walk today. Everything has sprung up so high that Harriet disappears completely as she bounces up and down through it all like an energetic gazelle. I call her and she races back as we come to the end of the long straight stretch. We round the last bend and there it opens out into the most beautiful clover walkway – an extraordinary sight, a definite pathway, with scrubland on one side about shoulder high and high grasses on the other, their pinky seed heads being crushed as Harriet dives into them. Here in the middle is a definite pathway carpeted with white clover flowers; a bed of blooms that seems to spring back after every footprint. It was about to be a really hot day, but here and now there was no strength in the early morning sunshine and yet it was warm enough to hold promise.

★ ★ ★

Something about coming across the surprise clover pathway in a field I thought I knew well reminds me of how we should never take anything for granted and how everything that grows is ever changing with the seasons. Because of that, it feels especially important to grab every view and every scent experience and hold on to it, even for a few seconds, before it's gone never to return in quite the same way or with quite the same meaning again.

I'm reminded of a piece of writing I did way back in 1973, when I was experiencing motherhood with my first toddlers.

On my Hands and Under my Feet

My twin boys were two years old and my eldest son three, and the kitchen floor was ankle-deep in toys and clutter as usual. A friend visiting today said, like so many others, "What a good idea having them so close together. They'll be off your hands before long."

I feel sad because I wonder if those who say it will ever realise what they've missed and thrown away by constantly rushing their infants through all the stages to that time when school and independence are there.

Okay, I can scream along with any mother at the end of a hectic day, when I just never seem to have enough hours or hands to cope – when I've thought that if that wail goes on much longer, or if I trip over one more toddler clinging to my skirt hem, they'll none of them reach their next birthday.

But with that never-ending trail of household chores that surrounds the under-five family and when I despair of ever finding a two-minute break to call my soul my own, there are so many compensations that I cherish because I know these experiences with my toddlers are all the more precious because they are soon gone forever. These days will never come again when, to my children, I am needed so acutely and so completely. To be able to bring a huge smile to a face with a great big kiss and a cuddle and to have podgy arms squeezing round my neck is indeed an intense pleasure.

I never drooled over other people's babies and even when I was pregnant, I often used to wonder how I would respond to my own. It was quite a revelation to find that, along with all the hard work, the pleasures followed in their multitudes. Snuggling a little body close and just holding something that seems to enjoy it so much compels one to join in and enjoy it too! I actually look forward to that cry in the night, just to get another look at him.

There are bad times along with the good: the bad temper, the tiredness, the times when you're ill and cannot cope and, worst of all, the worry. There seems to be a necessary agony of anxiety that accompanies having children. I can't believe I shall ever be quite as carefree again as before I gave birth; and yet will I really be quite so obsessed with whether or not to take him to the doctor with that cough, or whether or not to let him climb quite so far up that tree, and playing outside – he won't stray and get lost, will he? No, surely not. When they're teenagers I shall probably worry about whether they're safe on that motorbike and stay awake all night waiting for them to come in.

It seems to me that while we are tired and harassed, we should savour the good things that babyhood offers. The anxiety and the hard work make each pleasure so well earned that we should grasp it with both hands. It's like having a second chance at life, to see it all anew through a toddler's eyes: when to speak to a cat on the way to the shops is a thrill; and when talk of jelly for tea brings such glee to a small face that one feels guilty for ever wanting more from life than jelly.

I do have every sympathy with those who think children are at their most delightful all tucked up in bed fast asleep. What could be nicer? And while they're there, out of harm's way, I indulge in an orgy of adult satisfaction. And yet I have been known to prod one awake to get another hug for free.

One day there will be utter peace in the mornings and I shall stay in bed till lunchtime and maybe pluck my eyebrows as well; but then there will be no replete sticky bundle to give me a big wet kiss and say, "I do love you,

Mummy," and make me feel on top of the world. Tomorrow he could grow up and tell me he hates me!

Being a mother is something you don't have to do well to succeed in your toddler's eyes. Do the job badly and he'll still love you and give you another chance tomorrow. Who could ask for more in this success-orientated world we live in?

The position of 'mother' seems to have changed. It used to be regarded as sinful to go out to work when you had young children. Now, unless you carry on working until you go into labour and take up your career again before the baby is a month old (and, by the by, study for a degree as well), you're considered to be a rather brainless, drab cabbage.

It may be becoming rapidly antisocial to reproduce, and even more unfashionable to like being tied at home with toddlers, but while it lasts this is mine and I will enjoy it.

★ ★ ★

I turn to take one last look at the clover pathway. There is the fresh smell of dew trapped in the tightly bunched clover leaves. The sun will gain strength, the leaves will dry; it may never look quite the same again. I stoop to put Harriet on the lead before leaving and she rolls over on her back, waving her legs in the air, glorying in the softness of the clover bed – she too is grasping the moment – while this lasts this is mine and I will enjoy it.

★ ★ ★

It's 3.35am on February 10th 2008 and I'm up having a favourite milky coffee, silently wishing my youngest child, my daughter, a happy birthday. I'm unsure what has woken me but I move slowly and carefully to ensure Harriet stays fast asleep. Early morning walks I love but not 'in the night' walks. So here I am sitting alone at just the time Isabelle was born thirty years ago.

She was a beautiful baby from the minute she was born... the claim of all mothers. Again, in the quiet and alone I cradled her. Gorgeous auburn hair surrounded a very determined gaze, looking directly at me, staring attentively it seemed as I admitted out loud that I wasn't at all sure I knew what to do with a girl. My mothering skills were well honed on three boys, her brothers, but a baby girl...?

She was very special, totally unplanned and I'm still not quite sure how it happened! Even then, with the shock of discovering, somewhat late, that I was indeed pregnant, I had to smile at the way nature finds a way of defeating our exhaustive efforts to prevent such happenstances. This was 1977. This joyous surprise may have been unintentional but she was to be my last baby, cherished forever. Birthing was always an experience that reached my soul. Each time I felt I had touched the eternal... a feeling of utter bliss. This was fulfilment of purpose, uniquely mine, yet connecting with womankind the world over; a time to pity mankind that he will never experience this overwhelming ecstasy.

Is it this depth of encounter that programmed me and so bound me to each of my children that the struggle to recover their happiness after the divorce was fundamental to my very existence? Perhaps the strength of this bond was what made it impossible for me to grasp how their father was able to move forward and develop a life that included no meaningful contact with his progeny.

Birthing was at the heart of many a meaningful relationship for me as I undertook my work as a district midwife. Childbirth brings together both the heights of joy and the depths of anguish, with the midwife working with and through this gamut of restless emotion.

★ ★ ★

For some reason, I can't manage to sleep in this morning. Harriet has decided that, as it is beginning to get light, it's time to be up and out. I'm not

even managing to doze and can't block out her incessant whining, so I give
up and we are out by 5.45am; Harriet looking around, not quite able to
believe that all the other early dogs aren't out, raring to go, tails a-wagging.
It is raining drizzling rain; the sort that you think isn't really rain and will
stop any minute, but you're soaked in seconds and it continues relentlessly…
threatening always to stop, but never managing it. The rain rate increases to
a proper downfall now and I consider taking shelter in a lean-to cattle barn
as we pass. It's an open-fronted barn, so we slip in. We are both soaked and
I'm just thinking that maybe to stop was a bad idea and we'd be better to
push on home, when the downpour increases and the noise of the rain on the
tin roof of the cattle barn intensifies.

★ ★ ★

MARION AND JERRY

I remember weather like this at an even earlier hour, travelling with my midwifery bag and bedpan on the back of my 'sit up and beg' bicycle through the country lanes in Sussex with my dynamo light fading dismally if I didn't pedal fast enough. I arrived at a caravan in a soggy corner of a farm field and was welcomed aboard. This was an urgent call. I had not met the labouring mother previously… indeed I was soon to discover she had received no antenatal care at all. I was greeted by an anxious husband hurriedly motioning me up the steps and over the greyhound sprawled across the doorway at the top. The caravan was poorly lit by an oil lamp at one end as I made my way to the moaning sound coming from my right, mentally wondering how long it would be before daylight. The labour seemed to be well underway with only short breaks between contractions, during which I found I was unable to locate the baby's head in the pelvis and could only detect the heartbeat with the foetal stethoscope placed rather high on the abdomen. To be sure, and to determine exactly what labouring stage we were at, I needed to do a vaginal examination. I asked Marion's husband to please bring me the gas and air machine from the back of my bike. During my assessment, with husband hovering at a distance, I was not surprised to find that the labour was well advanced; the cervix was almost fully dilated. But I was concerned to learn that the breech was presenting through the neck of the womb at the top of the birth canal. (Babies usually deliver head first, this one was arriving bottom first.) While as midwives we did deliver breech births vaginally at that time, and it was not unknown for these deliveries to be carried out at home, it was seldom by design and certainly not without an antenatal history to depend upon. I swallowed hard, feeling thankful that at least it was a frank breech presentation – a bottom rather than a foot or knee. While determinably presenting an aura of calm reassurance, my stomach turned somersaults and sank to my boots as I tried desperately to ascertain exactly how many weeks pregnant she was while encouraging her to turn sideways on the makeshift bed adapted from the day-time window seat.

The rain was drumming loudly on the roof as the groaning escalated and I felt sure that that was the beginnings of a grunt I heard, indicating her need to bear down with the contractions. I needed to position her sideways on this bed and support both legs – one on the upended gas and air case, the other on a stool – so that I could have room and depth to suspend the baby's body below the level of the birth canal and wait patiently for precisely the right time to elevate the baby's legs and feet, allowing the baby's face to emerge, while controlling the slow delivery of the head. Struggling with lack of space and light, on my knees and trying to sound really calm, muttering what I hoped were reassuring words, something caught my eye just over my left shoulder, at the far end of the caravan. I momentarily pulled my attention away from my gloved hands and this slippery body to glance in the direction of the distraction. I was horrified to realise that the oil lamp had toppled over and the curtains were alight, with the husband seemingly totally unaware, transfixed by my activities.

"Excuse me… Mr Watts… I wonder if…" My voice came out at least an octave higher than I expected; all shrill and squeaky as though in need of WD40. Mr Watts was focussed on my every word; the problem being that the right words weren't flowing quite as they should. I suppressed a screech as I nodded in the direction of the flames… still no response. He clung to his wife's hand over the tumultuous contraction, for all the world wanting to help her through it. As her effort diminished, and the blessed peace of relief returned, the voice that broke the silence was Marion's. "Put the fire out, Jerry, there's a luv."

Thanks to Jerry and the rain, the flames were extinguished and the baby was born. As I laid him on Marion's tummy, he was still, quiet and very blue. I rubbed his chest vigorously and cleared the mucous from his mouth. I blew on his face and flicked the soles of his feet with my fingers. He and I took our first breath in unison, his loud scream followed, and in seconds his whole body flushed pink… all was well. I delivered the placenta (afterbirth) with some difficulty by torch light. And the downpour continued.

The beating of rain on a roof today brings the very taste of that experience flooding back…

The story didn't quite finish there I recall: the greyhound dog, who had seemed oblivious to all the goings on, came to life at this moment, pushing himself past me to streak off up the field in the rain with his jaws firmly clamped on the afterbirth.

7

THE STUFF OF LIFE: THE STORIES

We are so wet by now that I decide to push on home, doing my best to ignore the rain. I remove my glasses and hide them in my pocket… if only someone would invent windscreen wipers for spectacles. Harriet is looking very skinny; her soaking wet coat clinging to her body rather than it fluffing out all over as usual.

We hit the town and I momentarily consider hopping on the bus as it halts at the crossroads, but think better of it. Harriet is pulling away from it anyway, just in case it makes that awful noise with its airbrakes that frightens her so much that she hides behind my legs, tying my ankles up with her lead. We walk that last mile home with my mind returning to another time and another bus. It's thinking about that dog running off with the placenta that has triggered it…

★ ★ ★

"Is it true that once you left a placenta on a bus?"

It was to be a phrase that would haunt me throughout my career and was still reaching my ears right up to the time I retired. It was a story that refused to go away. Nurses I'd never met would greet me with it and always wanted confirmation of the rumour.

When, as a rural community midwife in the '60s, there was a need to go beyond your own borders to cover for a midwife in another area, it was sometimes necessary to get over there by bus. That ride had been necessary on this occasion. The labour had gone according to plan and now the delivery was complete, all except the task of dealing with the placenta. Once it had been checked and found to be complete (ensuring that uterine haemorrhage was now unlikely), it was the practice to burn it on an open fire. Failing that, it had to be buried in the garden. Neither of these strategies was possible on this occasion; there was no open fire, only a three bar electric heater, and being a very cold winter the garden was frozen hard and impenetrable for any spade. In these instances, the offending article had to be taken back by the midwife to be deposited in the cottage hospital incinerator.

All was going to plan until the comparative warmth of the homeward bound bus met with my fatigue and I fell asleep. Waking with a start at my bus stop, I hastily collected my delivery bag and gas and air case and leapt off the bus just in time. I was, at that moment, totally unaware of my faux pas and the placenta travelled on to the bus station depot. Little did I know then that the story was to travel much further…

That sinking feeling deep in the pit of my stomach returns as I remember sensing my career hanging in the balance when I was summoned to the midwifery superintendent's office. Once again I managed to live on through the crisis and by 'the skin of my teeth' was allowed to continue on, to bicycle another day. So now it's not only Harriet who shies away from buses; I've remained somewhat wary of them myself ever since.

When the memory of that fateful day raises its ugly head now, I take a certain amount of comfort thinking about the entertainment value the story has provided at many a boring dinner party.

I've been subjected to more than enough of those parties. The big disadvantage of attending such events on your own I've discovered, is that you are just bound to get backed into a corner by the most boring man in the room who wants you to see photographs of his cycling holiday in Norfolk. I'm learning to compete now with multiple pictures of Harriet walking nowhere in particular.

We go for an early evening wood walk today. Early enough to realise that the day isn't lasting as long as it did; it's late August. As soon as the longest day has passed, the mornings are slower to get going and the evenings begin not exactly to draw in yet, but hinting that they might soon. The lords and ladies (the wild arum) with their long straight stems and helmet heads of bright orange berries seem to know it too and are trying to shuffle into line either side of the footpath to brighten the almost gloom. The flower fairies poem about them jumps into my head…

Fairies when you lose your way,
From the dance returning,
In the darkest undergrowth
See my candles burning!
These shall make the pathway plain,
Homeward to your beds again.

(Cecily Mary Baker, 1926, Flower Fairies of the Autumn)

However, I'm not sure these lords and ladies haven't been to the party themselves; they look a bit drunk and like soldiers desperately trying to get into line but not quite managing it, with a threesome over there gossiping together instead of following orders. Their berries are shaped like the furry helmets of those guardsmen outside Buckingham Palace, but red instead of black, and they look weary with all the standing.

As we come up out of the wood heading for the common, there's the sound of a muffled cheer and a loud round of applause. The batsman will definitely be making an appeal for poor light. I reach the edge of the ground in time to see the players drawing stumps and returning to the pavilion. Harriet tosses her head as if in protest that anybody should dare to invade her ball chasing territory. Cricket pitches and weekends loom quite large in my memory…

★ ★ ★

My father played village cricket. I grew up believing that this was what every family did with its weekends: go to watch cricket, make the teas, put the tin numbers up on the board, collect six stones for the umpire to move from pocket across to pocket to count the balls of each over and, in later years, to score. These tasks were also known to extend to persuading cows back to their pasture and foraging in the undergrowth for the lost ball – all at the Chalfont St. Giles cricket field.

There is something so quintessentially English about village cricket and even now I can't pass a match, with its white clad players and the sound of leather on willow, without stopping to watch an over or two, whilst remembering the smell of newly mown grass and the taste of my mum's ham sandwiches, always prepared for the cricketers' tea.

★ ★ ★

RICKY

I sit on one of the benches surrounding the small common. It must surely be only just big enough for a cricket pitch; the boundary line is drawn directly in front of the seat. But since the game is now over we're not in the firing line and no great six ball thwack is imminent. I love this common in Chesham Bois. It forms part of so many of our walks, either on the way out or on the way back, because it's so near home. It is so much part of my life with Harriet. The cricketers begin to leave, with bats resting over their shoulders, chattering, laughing, dissecting the game, demonstrating the over arm googly that won them the match.

As I wait for the ground to clear so that I can myself lob some well chewed tennis balls for Harriet, I think of Ricky.

★ ★ ★

During my first nursing visit to Ricky I could tell he was a lover of cricket; a suspicion validated by the numerous books about cricket on the bookshelf behind his bed. It was a makeshift bedroom, adapted from his study when the need had arisen to move the bed downstairs.

Moving the bed downstairs is much more than a practical task when caring for people who are dying at home. When the patient can no longer manage the stairs, this expedient undertaking seems to take on a more sinister symbolism. It somehow compels patients and families to face the inevitable deterioration that's occurring; a decline that can be ignored while continuing with an increasing struggle to make it up and down the stairs.

On this occasion, the adaptation of the study into a makeshift bedroom seemed to be about something else as well. It was where the tragedy and Ricky could be shut away and forgotten for much of the time.

Ricky had a malignant brain tumour, and the treatment he had received had inflicted brain damage while rendering him severely paralysed down one side. He was now unable to speak and had a distant look that demonstrated how little understanding there was behind his eyes.

I tried but made little headway in developing anything of a connection with Sue, Ricky's wife. I was informed early on in my visits that this was a marriage in name only now and I wasn't to expect any hands-on help with Ricky's nursing care from her. I'm sure the devastation of what had happened must surely have entered into Sue's stance. I had hoped that, in time, I may have been able to gain a greater understanding of her position but, despite my efforts, it wasn't to be.

Meanwhile, Ricky lived a somewhat isolated existence in his adapted bedroom; always in bed, always, it seemed, alone, with the door closed. It seemed a drab, cheerless room. When I arrived in the mornings to prepare Ricky for the day, many times he hadn't even been given a cup of tea, or if he had it sat cold and untouched on the small table next to the bed. He was unable to eat or drink unaided.

The chatter from the young children getting ready to go to school never included a 'cheerio' or a wave to daddy as they dashed off. It was as if, having realised Ricky was not going to get better, he'd been written off; secreted into a corner like an unacceptable embarrassment to normal daily life. I'm sure it was Sue's coping mechanism rather than an intended affront or cruelty but nevertheless, the lack of engagement with Ricky by the family felt like both a failure on my part and a punishment inflicted on this crippled, dying man.

Daily visits with personal care tasks saw a relationship build between us. A professional relationship, yes, but caring brings in something else. Perhaps it's just plain humanity; one human valuing another for no greater reason than he's another human. I'm not sure what it is, but purely professional it is not.

At times, I felt sure there was a flicker of recognition from Ricky when I arrived and he seemed increasingly to follow me with his eyes as I worked; sometimes I'd be talking, sometimes there was silence.

It was a time when England was about to play Australia at the start of an Ashes test series and with an almost missionary zeal I decided Ricky was going to be up and dressed in his wheelchair, in the lounge, watching it. I hoped and thought he understood. I had learned to determine how and what he could comprehend and process and I felt, more than saw, his pleasure at my suggestion.

Things started well: blanket bathed, shaved, shirt on, underpants and trousers resting above his knees with Ricky perched somewhat precariously on the side of the bed, with me standing in front, astride his legs. My cricket banter, a one-way conversation, had accompanied all preparations. The next part of the procedure would necessitate me bear-hugging Ricky around his waist, with his partially good arm around my neck, and then lifting him to the standing position, his legs held firm by my knees, while with one hand I would reach down behind him and pull up the underpants and trousers before lowering him down again on to the side of the bed. From here, I would tuck the shirt in, do up the trousers, and position the wheelchair at right angles alongside the bed with brakes applied prior to again raising Ricky up from the front, swivelling him round and lowering him into the chair – a move not allowed now as the dreaded 'Health and Safety' forbid it! It's a tricky manoeuvre but one I'd performed many times in many situations over the years.

My arms in position, I began to count as I rocked Ricky; one, two, with an extra rock on three to gain additional momentum to pull him to standing... and he did indeed rise... and he continued to rise... and went on rising. At just the point when I realised that Ricky was much taller than I had appreciated when seeing him prone, I recognised I had passed the point of no return. Still clinging to Ricky, my arms locked around his waist, I felt myself pitching backwards, and as I landed flat on my back with Ricky on top of me, his underpants and trousers still around his knees, I heard the slam of the door as Sue departed.

I tried hard to breathe; all Ricky's weight seemed to be on my chest. With a feeling of panic overtaking the shock, I opened my mouth to speak when the miracle happened... Ricky laughed – a low almost growling chuckle, but it was an unmistakable laugh!

I eventually managed to ease myself out from under him, roll him over on to his back and support him with pillows. As I knelt on the floor next to him, helping him drink a much needed cup of tea, I fought back tears of joy as more random laughs just erupted from his usually expressionless face.

I'm at a loss to remember how I managed to get Ricky back to bed. I'm sure none of my manoeuvres appeared in any moving and handling text, but we accomplished it together. He was exhausted; it was clear that the intended event had now to be abandoned. Despite my failure to achieve what I'd set out to do, there was a lightness in my heart, and just a flicker of something in Ricky's eyes as he struggled to inch his partially good hand across the bedclothes to touch mine… it was as though he was thanking me for trying.

I took the newspapers in the following day, intending to show Ricky the sports pages and discuss the outcome of the day's play. The game had also been abandoned; not caused this time by my lack of expertise but by the incessant rain. The eyes in the expressionless face stared blankly at me. He needed something different from me today; he was tired and needed simply to be made comfortable and then allowed to sleep. No cheery one-way chatter today. I laid the newspapers aside. There would be another time.

After only a somewhat perfunctory wash and essential pressure area care, I sat next to Ricky, saying nothing while he relaxed and then fell asleep. I reflected on the ability to respond to the ebb and flow of patient need and how fundamental that was to the quality of good care.

Caring work is deeply thoughtful: yes, we do things for people; yes, all those technical skills are part of what we do, but true care demands so much more. It requires that we stand alongside those who are suffering, at times helpless as they are helpless, reaching across the unspoken gulf between us, silently using our presence to share something of their wretchedness.

This 'being there' is also a skill. It's the essence of what nurses bring to healthcare.

★ ★ ★

AMY

I notice all the bikes and their riders on our walk this morning. They're all arriving at the station ready for their early morning commute. Several of the bikes are chained in racks. Some look quite sporty with lots of gears; others look less loved, heavier, rather like the carthorse model designed for a job of work – sturdy and safe but rather slow. There is even one with a basket on the front that reminds me of the one I rode to school. There is no helmet attached to that one, while the gleaming, spritely streamlined one has a saddle that looks decidedly painful, with a smart aerodynamic helmet bolted to it. I tug on Harriet's lead as she hesitates and sniffs a particularly enticing tyre; the tug encouraging her to move on and resist the urge to pee on the most stylish, expensive looking bike in the row.

The bike rack, with its evenly-spaced bars, looks like a row of railings. As we walk on, I'm transported back to the 1960s and a previous row of railings at the far end of Portobello Road…

★ ★ ★

I leant my bike against the shiny, black, pointed railings and lifted the hinge behind the saddle to release my Gladstone bag. I pushed open the gate and began the steep descent down the steps to the basement.

No need to knock on this door. Amy would be expecting me. I reached through the letter box, withdrew the key on a string, unlocked the door and let myself in. I was washing my hands in the scullery sink when a cheery, "Is that you, nurse?" rang out from the next room.

I lifted the latch and stepped up into the kitchen. I reached into my pocket to retrieve a biscuit to placate the snappy mongrel who was being moved out of his favourite chair by Amy's insistent voice, as she waved her newspaper in the air. "Let the nurse git er bag darn, Oscar." The said Gladstone bag was not allowed on the floor and would always be placed on a double layer of newspaper, on the chair, in an attempt to avoid fleas and bed bugs; at the very least it was protected from the dog hair.

There was a huge stove in the corner of the room; a black enamel contrivance with a pipe climbing from the range up the back of the alcove and disappearing into the ancient chimney stack.

She was ensconced in her usual seat; a large, rather shabby armchair that seemed to struggle to cope with Amy's somewhat ample proportions. She reached down over the left arm of the armchair, retrieved a deadly looking metal handle, attached it to the front of the range and yanked open its door to reveal a roaring fire.

"Come over 'ere, nurse and git yersel thawed out. It ud freeze yer tits off art there today. Anyha, I got sumock to ask yer before yer get started on me today."

I held my hands out in front of the blaze, soaking up the warmth as I settled myself down next to the scrubbed table to listen.

Amy's stories often started in the middle; an approach to narrative I quite like. They were often fractured in terms of their sequence and she managed to somehow unwrap her conversations as though she was taking the paper off a sticky, chewy toffee. It took concentration to fathom the focal point of the tale and I sifted the dialogue as she nattered on, making sure I grasped the hub of her concerns.

We tossed our conversation back and forth over the next ten minutes as I boiled up my forceps in a saucepan on the range, took out my biscuit tin of baked dressings from the oven and got ready to do Amy's dressing; she talked and I listened. The discussion became stilted, somewhat artificial and unnatural, going round in circles. It was as though Amy was struggling to find the words for her question. I knew I must listen carefully, validate all that she was feeling, stay with it, and not be tempted to push her concerns aside by interjecting with erroneous reassurances.

As I removed the soiled dressings from the fungating wound on her right breast, the foul odour from the rotting tissue escaped into the room. I threw the exudate-laden wound coverings directly into the fire as inconspicuously as I could, and closed the door.

Amy had ignored the lump in her breast for far too long; in fact, for several months, and only gave in and called the doctor when the tumour had advanced, broken through the skin of the chest wall, was widespread and well beyond curative treatment.

Pauses became apparent in the stream of words and tears began to roll down Amy's cheeks as I worked. She inspected my handiwork and I pulled the jumper carefully over her head, trying to leave the coiled top-knot of silver hair in place.

Oscar returned to Amy's feet, waiting to jump back onto his chair as I began to repack my Gladstone bag.

Amy wiped her eyes with the handkerchief she had tucked up her sleeve, and I watched as she first bit her bottom lip hard then pulled herself to her full sitting height, carefully replaced the hankie, and locked a steady gaze on to my face.

"Well yer gotta tell me, Sister. No muckin' abaart. How long 'av I got?"

I dropped to my knees immediately in front of her chair and clasped both her hands in mine; her nails dug deep into my palms, her eyes stared so directly at me. This gutsy lady deserved the truth; it was now my turn to talk. Amy was listening. Amy was tough. I struggled, as so often before with a tough conversation.

I talked to Amy about what had made her ask me today how much time she had left, and what her thoughts were about that right now. All the while I'm assembling a collection in my mind of Amy's thoughts. It's crucial that I am sure how much she knows, while determining how much she really wants to know. What did she think might happen from here on in? Why was it important to know? Gradually, Amy voiced all her concerns. She wanted to know whether she would be able to stay at home. Whether there would be pain that she wouldn't be able to cope with. Had she got time to find a home for Oscar? How will it happen? Will I keep coming? I told Amy that I couldn't be sure how long she had, but that my experience would suggest that we were probably thinking in terms of several weeks, leading to perhaps several months. I paused. Amy waited. I continued, adding that it was probably unlikely that she would live beyond the end of the year, but I thought that for her to be here for the birth of her latest grandchild in a few weeks' time was a real possibility.

Relief spread over Amy's face as I reassured her about staying at home if she wanted to. Her grip on my hands relaxed as I explained the pain-relieving medication that would be available for her and that I would make sure she was not in pain. There and then we contacted the charity that would agree to take Oscar after her death; a big relief for Amy. Encouraged by my promise of support, of being there, she gave a sigh and asked if I would come back tomorrow when "Me kids'ull be 'ere, Sister, and u'll be able to 'elp me tell um, wont yer?"

I left, having made sure Amy understood that none of my estimates were definitive, that we would know more as time went on and that I would always be as truthful as I could if she wanted to ask me more.

Amy held her new granddaughter. She was quite poorly by then and she died later that same week. There is a picture in the family photo album of Amy in bed cradling the baby with all her folks present and toasting the birth.

Probably the most important discovery I made in the twenty years of working with those who are dying is that family intimacy, of a quality that may never have been previously experienced, is often possible around the time of death. What is important tends to change in the urgency surrounding the threat of death. Family values are refocused and differences can be resolved. Parties can be given the opportunity to speak from the heart; to share precious exchanges. Many times, it is the district nurse who is instrumental in making this family healing possible.

★ ★ ★

ANGELA AND EMMA

We walk back through the high street as we finish our walk today. It is one of those walks – a bit like driving home sometimes when you suddenly realise you can't remember doing the rest of the journey and can't quite believe you're there. I'm not really sure where we've been, but we're about a mile from home with Harriet leading the way. I glance at my watch and, yes, we've been out a couple of hours, so we've obviously covered quite a distance and, yes, I vaguely remember reaching down and clipping her lead on as we came out of the wood at the top of Rectory Hill, but how we got there is a bit of a mystery.

At the other end of the high street coming towards us is a young girl of about sixteen years of age, dressed in jeans and a t-shirt, with shoulder length hair bobbing up and down on her shoulders as she walks between her mum and dad towards us. I direct Harriet to make her go around them and they laugh as she does her best to trip them up with her lead. I apologise on Harriet's behalf and they move on, smiling happily. I think about another such family group...

★ ★ ★

Emma was on the big double bed, propped up against the pillows, next to her dad who was under the covers looking very pale against the crisp white pillowcase under his head. Emma had just had her sixteenth birthday and the cards were still up on the mantelpiece. She was reading the newspaper to Ray, her father. Emma was an only child, and Ray and her were very close and always had been, so Emma's mother, Angela, told me.

Ray had been determined to beat the leukaemia for almost a year now and had fought long and hard. He now looked exhausted and I remember thinking it was probably the birthday that had kept him going and how I needed to prepare Emma and her mother for the possibility of quite a rapid deterioration now.

Angela came in with coffee for us all and sat on the bottom of the bed, reaching her hand out to hold his and talking to me about how tired Ray was now. Together we talked about how things might worsen over the next few days, with Ray wanting to know;

wanting to prepare both himself and the family. Emma became quietly tearful and Dad, with effort, put an arm out to comfort her. Angela remained in control, as she had done throughout; always managing everything, keeping it all together, preparing nourishing little meals for Ray, plentiful clean bed linen, slippers ready with a warm dressing gown for when he needed help to the toilet. She seemed to be continually in control of all that was needed.

At Ray's funeral, Angela was physically supported by daughter Emma and could be heard throughout the ceremony openly grieving. Huge, distressed wails of agony rang out in the church. Young Emma was silent with all her energies going towards trying to comfort her mother. In the days that followed, Angela even needed to be helped to wash and dress, needed to be fed, and was sleeping only with the aid of sedatives. I was concerned about the amount of responsibility being shouldered by Emma and I managed to gather some family friends to help out with the physical help and care that Angela required.

I arrived one morning while one of Angela's friends was helping her with her breakfast. I took the opportunity to sit at the kitchen table and have coffee with Emma. Angela was needing so much time and attention that I felt I wanted to give Emma the opening to talk about her own feelings about the loss of her dad. She was struggling to say anything; to talk at all. There were long silences between us that hung there waiting to be filled. Emma finally managed to speak. What she said was not what I was expecting and forcefully reminded me of one of the real strengths of district nurse care: the ability to focus on the whole family care rather than just serving the patient in the hospital bed.

Emma said, "I feel as though I've lost my mother as well.".

This young teenager was indeed suffering a double bereavement – the mother she had known and relied upon was not there for her right now and, in reality, wasn't there for her for several weeks.

After tears and tissues, I suggested to Emma that she began a private diary, where she could perhaps offload some of her thoughts over this difficult time. I arranged to go back several times, not only to care for Angela but to spend time with Emma where she would choose something out of her diary that she wanted to share with me. I wanted to acknowledge her myriad of losses and to validate her raft of feelings. It enabled her to be angry with her mother for, as she saw it, letting her down when she needed her most. I was a 'safe' person to share angry feelings with, and maybe this played a part in enabling reparation of the mother and daughter relationship in the fullness of time.

Over time, I found that where patients had died at home and where I had been involved for several weeks or months, families appreciated a visit on the anniversary of the death. Very often, it allowed the partner of the deceased to go over again the happenings of those last weeks and days with someone who was there and who cared. Other friends and family members, many times, had expected all to be well by now and my reassurance that feelings and experiences that may still be strong, raw and painful were expected, were following a usual pattern and were okay, so often seemed meaningful.

There was something else that happened with the relationships I made with families over these times. These connections may have been very close at the traumatic times but after those first anniversaries of birthday, Christmas and perhaps the funeral were over, the dynamics of our relationship altered. Things began to readjust and, very often, meeting family members, maybe in the street, when things had moved on or situations had changed, brought a distance that wasn't an uncomfortable one but was clearly a reminder of another time and place. Not everyone wants to be reminded of those dark, unhappy days. So the goodbyes were said with warmth and thanks again, but with a sort of bitter sweetness that was happy to see me go. While this is exactly as it should be, I remember sometimes walking away with an empty feeling; a sort of regret that their relationship with me now only surfaced sadness for them.

In Emma and Angela's case, when I revisited many months later they were planning a day out together on the anniversary of

Ray's death. They talked about the ups and downs of the last year without him and how, when one of them was up, the other was able to gain support from them, and vice versa. Just as it should be, they were working it out together.

★ ★ ★

There are times when less off-road walking is a must. The mud is just too thick almost everywhere: boots muddy, trousers muddy, Harriet muddy right up to and including her undercarriage most days, followed by a workout getting her clean when we get home. So today we are walking the highway or rather the side streets, back streets and alleys surrounding the main thoroughfares, in an attempt to avoid the worst that the softer ground has to offer.

★ ★ ★

I have never known a district nurse who wasn't obsessed by street names. Having spent a lifetime looking for roads that don't exist on any map and that no-one but the postman has ever heard of, it's a difficult habit to break. House names continue to fascinate me, especially those that bear no relationship to the house or garden they attach themselves to. It was impossible to think that a house name would help direct you when you were in a hurry to make a visit. 'Tall Trees' would have nothing more than a scrappy bush on the landscape and 'Wisteria Cottage' would be a very large, three-storey barn of a place, with nothing more than pebbledash adorning its frontage. I've even found myself peering at road names while I'm on holiday.

Even now, I tend to remember people by remembering their addresses. Probably before I can recall their name, I'll remember where they live. It is all a hangover from working out a route to manage a daily list of visits on a bike, I think.

Shortly before I left my last district nursing post, a student I had with me for the day asked me how we managed on the district before we had mobile phones. This of course now makes community nurses so much more accessible. My student looked stunned when I told her about the small blackboard and chalk that used to be allocated with your district nurse uniform when I first started district nursing and midwifery. Having juggled your daily visit list, calculating both the distance to be covered, who was due to go into labour and the amount of pedal power time needed, you then wrote the addresses on your blackboard with an approximate time of attendance. There were still many homes without telephones in the middle '60s, so when his wife went into labour, the husband would either cycle or drive round to your home to view the blackboard in your window and then come to the address indicated to find you and to ask for your help. As more people had both landlines and cars, the list would be of telephone numbers rather than addresses.

It was in the late 1960s that I returned to Buckinghamshire to take up my district nurse/midwife post, serving all the outlying villages on the far side of Chesham: Cholesbury, Hawridge, Buckland Common, St. Leonards, The Lee and many more; a charming area. But I was highly relieved to be allocated a car – it was a very widespread district and all hills! I somehow felt I'd made it. The career I wanted *and* a car!

★ ★ ★

JIM AND BOBBY

We turn into a shingle crescent, running parallel with the main busy road, where the row of houses stands back with large gardens to the front and rear, and where there is a wooded area shielding them from the traffic noise. The houses are large and the gardens well-manicured. Harriet moves across from examining the thin strip of woodland to sniffing around an overgrown gateway. I draw level with her, to where I can see into the garden and see the house. While Harriet forages under a nearby bush, I can see the weed-covered driveway and, set farther forward than the others, the house looking run-down and uncared for. I know that had the district nurse been driving down this road peering at house names, looking for the address she had been called to, she would have looked no further. So often it is the case that houses and gardens requiring care contain people similarly in need. It begins to drizzle. I walk on, calling Harriet and tugging on her lead.

★ ★ ★

It was suggestive of so many homes I'd visited: once splendid, upright, proud homes, where occupants were now left alone, fledglings long ago flown, often one partner having passed away, with the sole inhabitant old, frail and barely managing, probably living in just one or two rooms.

Inevitably, it seems couples are always going to downsize 'when the time comes', but somehow it doesn't come, or rather they never recognise that it has already come. So often the time has come and gone, with the very thought of scaling down now seeming to be too big an undertaking. First the garden becomes too much to cope with and gradually becomes depressingly overgrown. Then the stairs become too much for one or both partners, each thinking, 'Well maybe we'll have a stair lift one day.' The problem is that you have to be as nimble as the people in the stair lift advertisements to be able to get on and off the contraption unaided, which means, in reality, you pretty nearly have to be able to manage stairs to be able to manage the stair lift. After all, those lively souls in the commercials could probably leap up the stairs two at a time!

Once the upstairs becomes out of bounds, the elderly person retreats into an ever-decreasing number of the remaining rooms, while at the same time often withdrawing into themselves as well.

Moving is eventually seen as too big a task to even consider and so the once beautiful home deteriorates. There's a sadness about the place… all its grandeur gone. The rundown appearance isolates it from the neighbouring residences, too often echoing the loneliness of its owner.

My mind wanders back to another dilapidated house…

Jim's house had certainly seen better days. Another sad-looking, rundown home, with plywood where the glass should be in the top panel of the front door and weeds climbing over the crumbling sill of the bay window to the right of what was once a porch.

My first call out to Jim was in response to a message left by the GP (General Practitioner): "Patient too dirty to examine. District nurse please attend." Jim was an eighty-six-year-old gentleman who lived next door to a pub where he spent a large amount of every day. He had large, weeping, varicose ulcers on both legs that required daily dressings. I did these every day in the pub snug bar for nearly six weeks, until I persuaded Jim to allow me to do the dressings at home. He was too frightened that when I saw his living conditions I would insist on a hospital admission or care home and there would be no-one to look after Bobby, a mongrel dog and his loyal companion (who drank nearly as much beer as Jim). While he was able to shuffle next door to the pub, life for him and Bobby held meaning. While washing my hands under the kitchen tap, I took a look in the fridge: half a tin of dog food lay next to a small piece of mouldy cheese. Because he could no longer manage the open fire with its back boiler, there was no hot water. A small, one-bar electric fire was sitting on the hearth. I'd never seen Jim in any change of clothes and I was unable to tell whether the dank smell of stale urine emanated from Jim or the armchair, or maybe even Bobby. Jim had long since given up climbing the stairs and so days and nights were spent here in the chair.

These were the days when 'home helps' were still in existence; those blessed persons who would shop, collect pensions, cook meals, walk the dog, befriend and who, alongside the district nurse, generally kept a watchful eye on those elderly persons who were just on the edge of coping, who really wanted to remain at home, but were only just managing to do so.

Meals on Wheels, a weekly bath (thankfully, Jim's bathroom was downstairs) and regular clean clothes did much to improve Jim's skincare and, together with some judicious continence advice, his quality of life improved; demonstrated by the smile on his face when he continued to visit the pub. This smile reflected the reassurance he felt, knowing he could remain at home and wouldn't be 'sent into one of them care places' because he couldn't cope and where he would have been forced to part with his Bobby.

I've always found it difficult to understand why, in the name of care, we advise, encourage, persuade, and at times insist, that the elderly go into a care home 'for their own good'. There often appears to be so little consideration for the myriad of losses this decision entails: loss of home, familiar surroundings, friends and acquaintances, maybe the only place of rest ever known, the self-determination to eat and go to bed at will. With this loss of independence and the strength of associated feelings, we then refuse to allow them to take their closest companion, their dog or their cat, dictating that it's not allowed. So many goodbyes, so much sadness, even anger, and no close mate to understand and to share all these changes with.

While we enact this abuse, we pretend to care. We fail at a deep level, somehow reassuring ourselves that our decision is the right one and 'it's all for the best'.

★ ★ ★

A beautifully snowy morning. My diminutive garden looks as well-manicured as any other when it snows; it may be a lie but I like it. I take pleasure in admiring the early blue clematis pushing its blooms out under the snow blanket draped along the high wall beyond the terrace. The wall is covered with climbing evergreens, all bowed down now with the weight of the snow that flurries down over Harriet as she brushes past.

On our walk Harriet delights in running backwards in front of me, catching the snow as it flies off the toes of my boots as I walk. We are the first visitors of the day as we head down into the wood; the virgin snow disturbed only by the bird footprints scattered ahead of us. The hilly field to the right awaits the shouts of joy from the children as they descend on their sledges; if the snow lasts, we might see snowmen tomorrow. We continue down to the footpath into the wood and as I follow Harriet's route through the snow around the bend at the bottom of the footpath, I remember snowy winters of my own...

★ ★ ★

There was the fabulous day when thick, fresh snow had fallen overnight and Dad decided the whole road should skip lessons and he spent his day weaving up and down our road in his car with everyone's sledge tied one behind the other on to the bumper; great squeals of delight peppered with screams of "Stop, stop!" when someone's rope broke!

He believed in fun did Dad, and an illicit day off school made it all the more exciting.

There was no health and safety. 'All schools close when it's cold' didn't happen in the '40s and '50s. We all walked unaccompanied to school, most of us some distance, in all weathers.

The big, round, boiler-type fire, encased in its own wire cage with its huge pipe ascending through the classroom roof, would be festooned after a playtime of snowball fights with an array of wet scarves, hats and gloves – also drying there would be Sissie Bradshaw's knickers. Presumably she did become continent by the time she left school. It was the weather for liberty bodices kept under the bed quilt overnight, with the vest still inside; all put on while still in bed in the morning before braving the cold of the bedroom. We heated pennies on the top of the small, round paraffin heater to melt the ice on the inside of the windowpane, permitting us to peer out.

★ ★ ★

As I struggle over the stile, Harriet darts underneath, scattering snow in a cloud as she rolls over in joyful mood. There was once another snow-covered stile and another time...

★ ★ ★

I had set off on my bike in the snow to a farm out in Sussex, about three miles from the town, and most of it uphill as I remember. I'd had a call from a phone box, from a farm worker living in tithe accommodation; a small cottage right out on the far edge of a large farm. I had visited mum for antenatal checks and knew just how far out they were. With the snow settling fast and the sky looking well laden with more, I was anxious to get there. John, her husband, had arranged to pick me up at the stile because it would have been difficult in the snow for me to cross the fields carrying a bedpan, delivery bag and the gas and air apparatus. By the time he got there, I resembled the abominable snowman and was pleased to scramble up onto the tractor seat for the final part of the journey. A warm kitchen welcomed me and, having established that all was well with unborn babe and mum, and that delivery wasn't imminent, we all huddled round the range with its roaring fire and drank tea with homemade biscuits for dunking. We continued to labour together throughout the rest of the day and into the night. It was all a bit slow but clearly progressing; this baby was just not that anxious to be born. Many cups of tea and several slices of the most delicious lemon cake later, he announced his arrival loudly, assuring us all that he had a good pair of lungs.

It was one of those good deliveries that went just the way it should: where the labour progressed slowly but surely; where confidence builds between parents and midwife, and where the wonder and joy at the birth of this new life will be remembered and cherished by all parties. I've only ever experienced this almost spiritual happening with a home delivery, where to share this intimacy of womanhood brings a closeness that makes the responsibility of the task an honour afforded to very few by way of the job they do.

The treasured recollection of the story is that I was snowed in and had to stay for a further two nights before the snow melted sufficiently for me to leave and reclaim my bike. With no phone in the house and snow above the windowsills, there was no choice but to sit it out and play nursery nurse. Indeed, I slept in the bed with mum, and the longsuffering John slept on the sofa and brought us both tea in bed in the morning! This event became a very special trophy for the memory bank, notwithstanding the two days' leave deducted from my annual holiday entitlement by the then area supervisor, namely 'she who will be obeyed'. I shudder to think what the layers of nursing management would make of such disgraceful behaviour these days.

★ ★ ★

Harriet barks, pulling my focus back to the here and now.

I say a silent prayer, giving thanks for central heating, as we start our return journey as more snow begins to fall. I can't feel my fingers as I reach down to attach Harriet's lead, and she gets impatient with me, snatching at snowflakes, trying to eat them all.

★ ★ ★

As we hurry on, I find other childbirth experiences fluttering through my head, together with thoughts about how very unusual it is now to find anyone who has had their baby at home.

There is always something special about a homebirth that I've never quite seen translated into the hospital context. Hospitals talk about birthing suites and try to have coloured curtains and birthing pools. However friendly and welcoming some hospitals have attempted to become, it can never capture the special quality of a homebirth.

We live in a society that has spent the last fifty years concentrating on institutionalising its deliveries and on frightening women into believing their very lives and those of their babies are being put at risk if they are foolhardy enough to consider a homebirth. Yet, I understand that, there are now discussions beginning to suggest that perhaps there is a place for home deliveries.

The real sadness is that we have allowed those special skills needed to manage a home delivery to disappear. We decided they weren't needed in the modern world. The skills demonstrated by midwives, who worked in the community for so long, were disregarded, and thrown on the scrapheap as outdated and of no value. The precious art of 'being with' and overseeing the natural birth day has long since been forgotten.

I wonder whether those discussing its possible comeback really understand the meaning of the home delivery. During a homebirth, the midwife becomes the couple's partner in a natural process, rather than the actively managed clinical procedure that birth becomes in hospital. I suspect that the belief held by those at present considering a return to home deliveries is that we need to convert the home into a technological delivery suite. That totally misses the point of what couples are really asking for when they choose a home delivery. The bonding of both couple and baby is about the whole birthing experience; not simply what happens at the time of the actual birth.

I'm reminded of how difficult it became during my last years of practice to hold on to the sort of death at home that people really wanted. When people are asked where they would prefer to die, most people want to die at home. When this want is questioned further, of course they want to be free of pain, which is as obtainable at home as in hospital. But more than this, I would discover that what they meant was that they wanted to die in their own bed, drinking tea out of their own cups and with their close family members beside them. Increasingly, 'the powers that be' with their 'health and safety' rules are insisting on turning the home into a hospital ward with hospital beds and hoists intruding on the image that patients and families hold of how dying at home would be enacted.

It becomes almost impossible to be unaware of how the intervention of the medical man, in both birth and death, has not only led to increased hospitalisation for both events but also in the escalation of intervention (some may say interference), particularly in childbirth. This may also be said to apply to a lesser but still significant degree, to the dying process.

Doctors deal with disease, and while it may be an overstatement to suggest that in the natural birth and death process he is perhaps superfluous, it's a view that is worth considering if the climate for childbirth is maybe changing and a return to home deliveries is a possibility. Alongside this, the idea that everyone needs to be admitted to hospital to die is also being challenged in some quarters, with care homes being encouraged to allow residents to stay with them within the care home situation to die, rather than scrambled to A&E (Accident & Emergency) when death appears imminent.

We have turned childbirth and dying into medical procedures that take place away from the home, in hospitals where professionals manage them as procedures. Yet these two happenings are emotional as well as physical experiences in which we will inevitably all be involved and which put meaning in all our lives, and yet we have somehow been led by the nose like cattle into institutions. Could it be that the tide is turning, albeit it ever so slowly, when district nurses and midwives will, once again, be at the forefront of both of these cornerstones of care; where the art of their craft correlates so well with all their technical expertise?

*** *** ***

We're walking along towards the common when my attention is drawn, as often before, to a big old rectory set back from the road, with a sweeping drive leading up to the front door. It has undergone the fate of many rectories, being no longer home to the rector of the local church; he now has a more modern private dwelling. When this rectory was up for sale, I remember inwardly mourning the fact that the one thing I had never managed in my career was to own and run a nursing home for elderly care. It was never a serious career consideration because I was never in a position to be able to purchase such a property but if I had been, I would have loved it to have been this old rectory. I wanted to call it 'Bedside Manor'.

Harriet always snuffles in and around the border hedge here in front of the rectory. I'm never sure why but clearly there must be something of particular interest, or maybe it's simply that a couple of years ago she suddenly dived in right here and returned with a snack-sized pork pie that had to have been discarded the night before on the way home from the pub!

The way the sun is coming up behind the building creates a silvery glow that seems to be creeping over the roof. It looks like a picture postcard as we walk by.

★ ★ ★

MARY AND TED

Mary had only recently gone into the care home; she had been nursed at home for several years until Ted, her husband, had no longer, even with our support, been able to manage at home. Mary had been diagnosed with Alzheimer's dementia many years ago and now she no longer recognised Ted and had begun to fear him as though he were a stranger. Ted himself had begun to lose his eyesight and when he had been admitted to hospital for an operation, Mary had gone temporarily into a care home. Surprisingly, she had settled really well and seemed much less anxious and more content than she had been at home of late.

Despite this, it was difficult for Ted to decide to leave her in care when he returned from hospital. He knew his eyesight was going to continue to deteriorate and here he was, eighty-seven years old, needing to learn coping strategies for himself, yet tearful about leaving Mary to be cared for by others.

He explained how loyal Mary had been to him in the war, and how friends had come home after the war to find their wives had 'gone off with those Yankees'. He went on to talk about his ship being bombed and spending hours in the water waiting to be rescued, thinking of Mary and how he had vowed to care for her forever.

Ted said that watching Mary deteriorate, as the dementia had progressed, had been like losing her bit by bit. He spoke of unending grief with each backward step she took; each thing she couldn't do anymore became a loss for him too.

I was going in to see Mary in the home to be sure she was continuing to settle and also to offer any help to the care staff on her behavioural needs with the experience we had gained over the years while nursing her at home.

As I entered her room, she was alone sitting in her own favourite armchair with her head resting in her hands, hiding her eyes. As I sat down next to Mary, I spoke and she raised troubled eyes to look at me. She shook her head slowly for several minutes telling me, "It's all very confusing... the world's all upside down."

I took her hands in mine and talked about the changes, trying to highlight the things that had stayed the same for her: her breakfast bowl she had on her lap, her favourite cuddly toy that I placed in her hands. But nothing seemed to be working. Mary continued shaking her head and repeating that it was all upside down. I struggled on, not making much progress, when I noticed that Mary was staring, her eyes fixed on her bedside clock with tears beginning to run down her cheeks.

I too looked at the clock and then exclaimed, "Is it the clock, Mary?" as I hurried to reach and turn the clock over, to turn it the right way up. I then smiled as a look of calm spread over her face and she returned to eating her cereal. The world was all right again for Mary.

I said goodbye and went to see the carers to commend them on how well Mary had settled in such a short time. I also wanted to share some of Ted's worries because I knew that these carers, who were so committed to their work here, would also be able to support him when he visited Mary.

While there are really good care homes like this, where patients live happy, satisfied lives, and where caring, dedicated staff enjoy their work, sadly that isn't always the case. Residential care homes and care agencies providing care in patients' own homes both struggle to meet the needs of vulnerable, elderly people. Until, as a society, we decide we want to not only value our elderly but also to value those who care for them, then the quality of care they receive will continue to depend on how much any recipient is able to pay to be helped to the toilet.

With the predicted rise in the number of people who will suffer from dementia in the coming years, we will need every one of our devoted carers and many more of them.

8

HARRIET AND ME

A lovely walk today. Only two weeks after all the snow and very cold weather, it's really mild. As we enter Jacob's Ladder Wood, there is the drumming of a woodpecker right above us. I look and look from all angles round the bottom of the tall tree that I know he must be in. I can hear him so clearly but I can't manage to catch even a glimpse and Harriet is running back and forth, desperately telling me to move on and watch her carry sticks instead. As we turn left onto the bridleway at the bottom and begin the long trawl, slowly climbing up the slope, there, on the right, I suddenly see the sharp, dark green spikes pushing through the old fallen leaves on the bank – the very beginnings of the wild crow garlic. I can't be quite sure what it is until I crush two of the baby, spiky, grass-like leaves between my fingers… and, yes, it really is. Last year I looked forward every morning to reaching this bit of the walk; the fragrance of the garlic would greet me before I could see the bank, calling me on with its heady scent, until suddenly, there it was, a mass of tiny white flowers bathed in this glorious perfume, so sweet, so much more gentle than its cultivated brother.

I love this wood, especially on a really hot day. It's cool and shaded within. It is said that the steps down – the ladder – were once at the beginning of the garden of Mr. Jacob of 'cream cracker' fame. This was all his garden I understand. I silently thank him for sharing it with Harriet and me.

This time last year, Harriet had struggled to make it up the bank, whereas today she bounds up there, sniffs around in the young shoots and then gallops off to investigate another smell; one much more interesting to her nose than simple wild wood garlic.

★ ★ ★

I think about this last year with Harriet. I am still amazed at how much a part of my life she has become, just how much joy she brings me and how much we share.

What has she taught me, this four-legged friend of mine? What are the gifts she has given me? I began to think about her loyalty. I can always count on her welcome. Whether it be when I arrive home or when I return to the car from a shop, her focus will be entirely on me, even when I can't see her clearly because of the picture painted on the windscreen by the reflection of the trees. Her gaze will not falter. Whatever sort of day I'm having, she will overwhelm me with her enthusiasm; she never fails. As I think about how people change, relationships fail, and friends let you down, she is my constant; my dependable companion. As I grow older and the world moves faster, her quality of steadfast loyalty and trust is humbling. She depends on me to feed her, walk her, care for her and she repays me with her heart and soul – these are my gifts – gifts she gives without measure. These treasures are communicated to me without reserve. What she means she says clearly.

When I say she never fails, I will always remember when she demonstrated such sensitive understanding of something that was happening to me that even now I am quite moved when I recall the incident. We were away staying with friends for a weekend and I became quite ill – it turned out to be a rip-roaring throat and ear infection but it began with me feeling really feverish. I took the earliest opportunity I could to retire to bed with Harriet sleeping on the floor beside me. I was restless and so very cold, I was shivering, with my teeth constantly chattering, despite hot drinks and more blankets. Finally, I got out of bed and put my tracksuit on over my PJs in an effort to get warm. I was miserable and wretched and feeling very sorry for myself. I wanted to be at home in my own bed and, most of all, I wanted to get warm. If only I could get warm, I could sleep.

Harriet sat looking up at me for several minutes, her gaze steady and almost enquiring. She then performed her little miracle. She jumped up on the bed, pawed at the bedclothes to pull them back and buried herself under the covers laying right alongside me; pushing close up to my body with her head on the pillow next to mine. The warmth from her body immediately began to soak into mine and as she lay so still and settled, the comfort of this 'human' hot water bottle at last brought me sleep.

Harriet has never, before or since, even stayed on the end of my bed. She jumps onto the floor when I go to bed. She won't even sleep in any dog bed. She's never once attempted to get under any covers. But that night she stayed there, never moving, until I got up in the morning and released her. Without delay, she headed for the water bowl and drained it, desperate to slake her thirst before heading out to the garden.

I've heard about dogs that perform enormous feats of bravery for their masters; digging them out of snow drifts, or swimming out and saving a drowning child. I've always been in awe of such apparent intuitive abilities. Not for us those dizzy heights for sure, but something almost beyond explanation happened that night; maybe it was simply some duty Harriet, the working dog, felt she had to perform to make things better, perhaps?

I'll never know how she knew what I needed or what instinct directed her to do what she did but one thing I do know for certain... she heard what I didn't say and she answered what I didn't ask.

PETER AND PADDY

This memory of what felt like love and care from Harriet to me takes me back to another dog and another occasion.

I'd been asked to visit a young man in his twenties who had recently had an operation for cancer and had been discharged home from hospital the day before. The GP had asked me to visit to start a course of injections for Peter and had told me that he thought that Peter was living with a girlfriend.

I arrived at a semi-detached house with two doorbells, indicating there were two flats inside. It was a dull, grey, drizzly morning. Peter opened the door in his dressing gown. He invited me through a door at the bottom of the stairs leading up to his flat. As I reached the upstairs hallway (in effect the landing), Peter indicated that I needed to mind a rather old, tired looking Labrador lying just inside. I stepped over him and then followed Peter silently down a cold, dingy hallway to the kitchen where he was putting on the kettle.

We moved into the front room and seated ourselves either side of a wood burning stove set into an old existing fireplace. Burnt out ashes remained in the grate of the stove – there was a cheerless feel throughout and Peter was hardly uttering a word. I was struck by the emptiness. This was a flat clearly being decorated. The wallpaper was half stripped from the walls. It looked like a project in progress; a couple setting up home together.

However, an air of misery seemed to bounce back at me from all directions. I sat holding my coffee cup on my lap, with a pale-faced Peter barely responding, giving monosyllabic come-backs and leaving my enquiries floating unanswered to the floor.

As I worked at it, looking in from other angles, trying different approaches, I could see Peter fighting to hold back the tears as he buried his face in his hands. As I moved forward to be close to him, to put my hand on his, the old, very arthritic dog from the hall tottered in and pushed himself between me and Peter, placing a favourite soft toy in his master's lap. Paddy thought I was the cause of his master's upset and he'd come to protect him, deliberately putting himself between Peter and me; almost pushing me away. What devotion. Peter and I both smiled, and we got started.

Peter had presented at the doctor's surgery with a lump on his shoulder. He had noticed changes in one of his testicles some months previously, but had done nothing about it; he'd let it go, not wanting to go to the doctor with something so personal and private. The lump on his shoulder was a secondary deposit. The cancer had spread.

He began to tell me that his girlfriend was so angry that he had, as she saw it, cared so little for her, that he had risked everything by not responding to signs and symptoms earlier. He told me that she had refused to visit him in hospital, and when he'd arrived back home yesterday they'd had an angry row and she had packed her bags and left.

Here was this young man alone, frightened and bewildered, facing an uncertain future and soon to begin a course of gruelling chemotherapy treatment with no close support.

As we talked, Peter reasoned that the cancer and its treatment was surely sufficient punishment for his failure to attend to the first symptoms of his disease; his rhetorical question hung in the space between us…

The next three months were hard for Peter but he had a good prognosis and he did well. We had many much easier talks over the following weeks, with Paddy (the dog) never really making friends with me. He would always sit right next to Peter throughout my visit as if to warn me not to upset him again!

Quite some time later, I did see Peter in the local high street, looking much happier; holding hands with a girlfriend and laughing and chatting. I don't know whether this was his previous liaison or a new relationship but either way it was good to see life moving forward for him.

I was very touched to receive a case of twelve bottles of red wine at my retirement party, with a card from Peter saying there was one for every one of the twelve worst weeks of his life, to say thank you for my support. I wasn't sure that Paddy would have agreed to me being given such a generous gift!

Harriet runs ahead in her usual carefree mood and I lengthen my stride just a bit, realising my feet are wandering like my mind and my pace is only just above a dawdle. All these thoughts about my relationship with Harriet have led me on to think about all those different relationships that happen throughout our lives…

★ ★ ★

Relationships have always been important to me, whoever they are with; they are what is important in my life. The way we communicate and what is shared between two people, I believe, is the basis of all great friendships (and what is life without those very treasured friendships?). So the qualities of exchange and interaction, I believe, were at the heart of my nursing career, my practice and my lecturing – abilities so often undervalued: the ability to gain access to a patient's home who needs but doesn't want you there; the ability to fit in 'when in Rome', the ability to motivate nurses with teaching that inspires them to give of themselves, the ability to recognise the essence and value of nursing care, and the ability to ensure the memory of what you say remains with them. This all relies on the ability to communicate well at a real level.

Harriet is a clear communicator: wag your tail if you like someone, go towards them and lift your paw to touch them; if you don't like them, growl, back off and bare your teeth! It maybe somewhat simplistic but never are you left in any doubt as to what the dog means. How often do we humans say one thing but our body language or eye contact says something entirely different? How often, when someone is talking to us, are we really listening? Or are we simply waiting for them to stop so that we can have our turn?

Very early, and in the almost pitch black, I've finished the New Year's Eve night shift volunteering at Samaritans; a shift full of heavy duty listening. Harriet greets me as though I've been away for at least a month and can't quite believe it as I reach straight for her lead and ball thrower. No waiting while I do boring things like sinking into a chair – just up and off; great! I fancy that if I sit down the eyelids will instantly close after the long, demanding night. I head for Hervines Park. Feeling that it is just too early and gloomy for woods and footpaths, we road-walk our way there and the darkness does just begin to lift a very little by the time we reach the open ground. The ball is hardly visible as I fling it across the uninhabited football pitch; the only visible signs of life being flashes of white fur as Harriet streaks after it. I get into a monotonous rhythm of throwing, and she responds with chase, fetch, return to my feet, drop and run again… throw, chase, fetch, return, drop and run. This could go on for hours.

★ ★ ★

My mind returns to my night. There was nothing different from most other nights and yet it was as exceptional as every other night; a night where again I'd been afforded the opportunity of entering into the lives of others. When a caller chooses to share deep feelings, to be able to be alongside in their darkest moments is a privilege to be truly valued, however sorrowful the story.

Alongside exceptional volunteer colleagues, there is a shared honesty about why we're there and why we're supporting each other. Defences fade away in the face of the misery of human experience laid bare. I guess we leave every shift recognising the power of what we're struggling to do with a heightened awareness of who we are. Juxtaposed with all that suffering, the insignificance of our own problems feels palpable.

New Year is traditionally a time for reflection for most of us but any thoughts of New Year resolutions just dissolve against this backcloth. Yesterday, I was feeling a bit like Bridget Jones, wanting to record how many calories I'd ingested and what my daily thigh measurement was, together with how many more lines have developed on my face overnight. Added to that, I thought I might decide to paint my toenails more regularly…

This morning, even this early, before the cold light of day, these trivialities seem so insignificant I'm almost ashamed to have thought them worthy of any consideration.

How lucky I am to be here with my loyal companion, with a family that cares, with a home to go to and a cup of coffee waiting to be enjoyed.

My mind unexpectedly makes a connection between my feelings of fortune now and those I often experienced at the end of a day's work, reviewing my patient visits and finding myself thankful that today *wasn't* the day that I had received confirmation myself of a life-threatening diagnosis.

I'm not quite sure what meaning is held in that connection but clearly, even in a voluntary capacity, I have a need to try to help those in a less good place than I find myself. Maybe it's simply a need to be needed or perhaps, more pertinently, I get something from the outcome. It is the payback, the satisfaction I gain from the care I give, that feeds the inner me at quite a profound level. There is also a sense of me paying back, or giving back; the sort of barter system of contribution to society that enables the circle of humanity to keep going.

I believe that the changes happening in nursing are destroying that job satisfaction: the payback. Towards my retirement, I constantly felt I was involved in less and less direct patient care, staying longer and longer at the computer carrying out management requests – tasks that didn't serve the patient. Indeed, most often, they just took time and visits *away* from patients and provided numbers and jobs for increasing layers of management personnel.

★ ★ ★

Bright, bright sunshine this morning as soon as we set off. The sun is so low in the sky that I'm forced to keep my eyes focused on my shoes. It's a weak sun with no warmth behind it as yet. I turn off into the wooded part of the walk and the sun shifts to my side. Very often on the early morning walks there are 'the worker walkers' – those of the rapid pace; fitting in the dog walk before running for the train and the office. But we're a band of brothers, those of us out and about while others lie abed; the fellowship of the dawn dog walker. This sense of congregation is heightened when we bump into one another in the darkness of an early, cold, frosty winter morning, or dog leads become entwined as our charges exchange bottom sniffs. We owners get no more intimate than to simply nod to one another in recognition of our hardy, intrepid disposition; comrades against the elements. We greet one another with a fulsome 'morning' and even a raised gloved hand. Some are even dressed for a day in the office but with Wellington boots and a cagoule over the smart suit, but more often it's a pair of baggy tracksuit bottoms pulled on over the pyjamas; a precursor to the shower on returning home.

The strange thing is that as the day moves on, even this level of familiarity amongst the owners seems to wane and it can become something of a challenge to engage in even dog talk on the street, let alone chat.

And then, of course, there are the joggers and runners, most with a mutt of some description in tow somewhere. I always feel a bit sorry for these dogs because it is most probably their only walk of the day and what about all that sniffing and stopping and peeing on certain tufts of grass to let your friend know you've just passed by? Surely every dog owner knows that this is just so important to every hound. How do you manage to fit that in if you're attached by a lead to a man who appears to be running for his life, puffing and blowing the whole way with a special water bottle in his other hand, arms pumping backwards and forwards like pistons? Even when he's only jogging, rather than really running, it's a struggle. Harriet and I wander rather aimlessly along while the black Lab over the road looks across longingly at us as if saying, "Hiya! Sorry can't stop; we've got another four miles to go at this pace before he goes to work... bye!"

★ ★ ★

Quite late in my career, at fifty-four years of age, I became a lecturer at The Royal Marsden, which necessitated awful commutes into London on the early morning train. Commuting by train is a whole new world!

A deafening silence descends, except for the odd mobile phone call. All travellers should be congratulated on their ability to avert their gaze, regardless of the havoc taking place.

I had a nosebleed on one such journey and was trying to retrieve a packet of tissues from my briefcase with one hand, while managing, with considerable difficulty, to stem the flow with the napkin from around my paper coffee cup. All newspapers were lifted a little higher while various members coughed and fidgeted, trying to pretend they hadn't noticed. I was so tempted to reach out and grab one of the displayed white handkerchiefs in those 'oh so neat' top suit pockets but I feared it might make the front page of tomorrow's newspaper to be so brazen. The same people travelling on the same train, day in day out; why does no-one speak? What a huge missed chance to interact with others; great conversations and friendships. When John Donne said 'No man is an island' he had obviously never travelled on an early morning commuter train.

I smile now as I muse on the wide variety of human relationships we all do and do not develop in our lifetimes... particularly those relationships with patients; some close and some simply professional.

★ ★ ★

Harriet bounces back from the undergrowth to jump up and leave two muddy paw marks on my tracksuit. It's as if she's reminding me of my relationship with her.

★ ★ ★

The relationship between a dog and a human is always complicated. The two know each other in a way no-one else quite understands; a connection shrouded in personal history, temperament, experience, instinct and love.

This sense of deep companionship between owner and faithful hound can be strange to explain; a relationship that doesn't depend on the dog's qualities or merit but rather on some bizarre and subtle coming together of like-minded spirits. Maybe it is this 'spiritual knowing' aspect that is the essence of the value held between us and yet, while I hold fast to this satisfying feeling of partnership, I know that I don't readily acknowledge its depth to others. This may be because the profundity of the relationship between man and beast also carries with it a level of embarrassment, since we dog-owners know deep down that the sense of adulation is not only one way, not only from him to you, but that you're definitely an equal party in this mutual admiration society.

I read the strapline on a card I couldn't resist buying recently, which had a picture of a quite ordinary dog on the front. The dog was staring up adoringly at his owner. Written underneath was:

'Do not accept your dog's admiration as conclusive evidence that you are wonderful.'

Why not, I say; it feels okay to me. I might paste it onto my fridge to remind myself of how wonderful she thinks I am!

★ ★ ★

The last couple of weeks in January seem unending this year. The winter landscape is drained of colour. The woodland seems lifeless and the trees stand bare; their skeletal silhouettes stark against the dull grey skyline. Harriet enjoys drinking from the many tree roots harbouring the results of a night of heavy rainfall but it's just a steady drizzle now, and over the last few weeks I've learned to be grateful for such small mercies. Last year the hazelnut catkins had begun to show by late January. Today I see no sign of any. The mud continues to deepen and I choose to stick to the main bridleway, rather than go off track up over the field. It's just too sticky to get a firm foothold and galloping full tilt and sliding to a standstill, spraying mud in all directions, is a talent Harriet has perfected but I have yet to learn.

We come to the fallen tree obstructing part of the bridleway. It's been there some time now and a pathway has developed around it with moss and toadstools taking hold along its length. The rain has found and formed a riverbed of its own around the rotting trunk, taking leaf debris on down the hill. The extent of the rain is quite altering the trail terrain; the rivulet carving its path all the way down and under the railway bridge at the far end.

Even Harriet seems fed up with the unremitting rain. It seems to have gone on forever, adding another chapter to each and every walk. When we get home, there's my dirty boots and her muddy paws, all the way up to and including her underbelly. It's like an extra workout getting her clean and then making sure she doesn't decide to dry herself by rolling on my bed.

She always looks so dejected when she's wet and I'm musing about how similar her expression is then to Deborah's now as we meet on the common. Max, her black Scottie dog, sits quietly by her side looking depressed while Harriet finds a particularly large, muddy puddle under the park bench and begins to splash about and dig. Deborah doesn't really like Harriet. She looks at her disapprovingly and always backs away, wary that she might jump up. Deborah doesn't wear dog-walking clothes like the rest of us. She's always got matching gear on: leather gloves and swanky leather boots; not for her tracksuit trousers and a fleece with dog treats in the pocket but rather a smart jacket with a fur collar, and always an immaculate hair-do. She begins to drone on about her longing for grandchildren and her daughter's refusal to oblige. I try to make sympathetic noises but I'm aware that they don't sound too sincere. It seems to be a necessary accompaniment that develops in the newly retired and it's one I neither understand nor share. The strange thing is that many of these wannabe grannies seem to have missed the delights of their own children as preschoolers, busy being the emancipated women who have it all, career and model mum. Could they now be hankering for what they missed?

Deborah then begins to bleat about the fact that they've had to postpone their 'little break' in Cyprus because of her husband's work – important city *gent, I'm not sure what he does exactly, and possibly neither does Deborah, but of course he's far too critical for them to manage without just now and she so needed that little break. It's over three months since they got back from skiing in St Moritz.*

★ ★ ★

Perhaps it's just me who's missing the 'longing to travel' gene. If you're on your own and retired, it seems everyone thinks you're desperate to stand in Tiananmen Square or to cross the San Francisco Bridge. When Harriet and I holiday, we head for Cornwall with its indeterminate weather, coastal walks, beaches with sand dunes and fantastic cream teas.

★ ★ ★

It begins to drizzle quite heavily and Deborah of course has her umbrella, but now takes her plastic rain hat out of her pocket as well. She then dictates that I must take Harriet home and bathe her. I have a really nasty thought running through my head; I want to tell her to take miserable Max home and maybe put him down and get a more cheerful dog… but I don't. In reality, I stoop and ruffle the fur on Max's head and silently tell him to cheer up as I give him one of Harriet's favourite treats from my pocket when Deborah isn't looking. Max is on a very special vegetarian dog food and is not allowed any 'extras' I've been told.

As Harriet and I head for home, I look down at myself and realise just how shabby my dog walking clothes are and, yes, I too will need a bath.

★ ★ ★

How glad I am to be living with only Harriet. A woman doesn't have to worry about looking her best to impress a dog: no make-up, tousled hair, scruffy shoes; she doesn't care. Harriet knows I'm beautiful because I have a ball in my pocket.

9

MY NEW PASSION IN LIFE

I pull into the field and leave the engine running while I close the farm gate. I then jump back into the car and head down to the far end of the field to park up where there is shade under a mulberry tree that is just coming into fruit. Harriet tramples back and forth across the back seat, whining with excitement and putting her front paws up on the inside door handle and poking her head impatiently out of the half open window on either side in turn, looking, looking again; where are the sheep?

★ ★ ★

We have together found a new passion in life: sheepherding. Neither of us is brilliant yet but we share an eagerness in the craft that must surely yield results in time through sheer determination. I recall my excitement as I woke this morning to find it was a sheepherding day – like a child who remembers today is his birthday!

★ ★ ★

Pam waves from the other field and I wave back, trying to look vaguely more controlled than Harriet. Gordon shouts, "G'morning," as he disappears driving the truck with the hay bales through to the far field. Between them, they run their small sheep farm and, alongside the work that entails, they allow novices like me access to their sheep; helping both the dogs and their owners.

★ ★ ★

I can't quite believe the fascination, the wonder, the desire to learn more, and just the sheer joy that I have found in this newest pastime. To watch a sheepdog learn to gather a flock of sheep, execute the lift, and fetch them back down the field is like watching a talented musician extract incredibly beautiful sounds from his instrument.

At our first lesson with Pam, Harriet was backing off on to the pen railings as the sheep did their best to frighten her – turning and stamping their feet at her while they tried to knock me over in the mud – and the rain poured down. I remember thinking that if I could enjoy this now, it held something special. It did too. We moved on to the glorious spring weather, with its lambing, its learning and its laughter.

Friendships have grown with other Collie dog owners learning to herd. They have your true Border Collies – the ones seen on *One Man and his Dog* – so Harriet with her long shaggy coat doesn't quite fit the image. But Beardies were used for herding in the past. Harriet grew in confidence, became excited about herding and I began to learn not only about sheepherding but also about sheep.

I'm filled with wonder at what Harriet is capable of doing even now, and it's so rewarding training her and watching her develop. I've allowed myself to believe that if I can train her to go to the end of a large field and bring a hefty herd of sheep to me, maybe even with whistle commands, it will be one of the great achievements of my lifetime. We haven't reached the dizzy heights of the whistle yet; we're working with our 'comebye', 'aaway' flanks, and our 'walk on' verbal directives for now.

And above it all it is profoundly pleasurable to find that, in retirement, there is something that sets me alight with a new dream, especially when it had never registered on the radar of 'things I want to do'. There are, inevitably, interests developed when you give up work that you've waited years to have time to do and that's great, but this is something different: a world about which you had no notion reaches out and grabs you, forcing you to take notice and to respond to its lure.

Sadly, what usually runs right alongside beginning these long-awaited leisure pursuits is a huge frustration at not having somehow tackled each and every one of them earlier. Maybe I would have discovered some hidden, previously unexposed, talent that I would have been able to reveal to the world... yes, well, don't let's get carried away.

At times now it flashes through my head that maybe I chose the wrong career and should have gone into sheep farming instead. I'm not sure it's a really serious thought and maybe it's just a desire for another 'crack of the whip' or perhaps, more pertinently, to have another chance to get it right. But the thing we don't have by the time we reach retirement is the time to try too many different things and get them wrong... well, big things anyway. The young have the advantage of all those years ahead when any bad choices can either be turned around or at least discounted by the good choices made later; when mistakes can be followed by victories. Perhaps as we get older we are just less willing to take chances. Maybe we become somewhat risk-averse while the young have a more 'gung ho' attitude still going on for them.

I feel sure we all have an unclimbed mountain within us waiting for us to plant our own Union Jack on its peak. I'm not sure I'll ever stand at that post, crook in hand, with Harriet translating my every whistle like a linguist and penning her sheep like a winner, but I do know that sheepherding and trialling is rapidly becoming my unclimbed peak!

★ ★ ★

We walk over to the enclosure where six sheep cluster together awaiting their fate. Harriet, with great effort, manages to restrain herself and stays close by my side with pertinent reminders from me at regular intervals. She's crouched close to the ground at every step; head forward and low, eyes directly on the sheep, tail down, one front paw hovering above land in typical sheepdog pose. This stealthy stance is repeated with every step until we reach the gate. The pen is large, about thirty feet across, and I direct Harriet to lie down outside the gate while I open it and step inside before allowing her to join me, again with the instruction to lie down. She must wait to be invited to the sheep by me. We start working together, with Pam leaning on the gate shouting instructions:.

"Back out… back out. Keep her back from the sheep. Don't let her circle the sheep like that! Lie her down…. now, walk on. Let her balance the sheep! Keep going… let her work! That's better."

So we're not quite poetry in motion yet!

We work on, Harriet and I, both trying hard to get it right. It's a hot day and the sheep need a rest. I instruct her to lie down once more and go towards her with a "That'll do," accompanying the slap on my thigh as I take her away from the sheep. I continue to exhort her to stay at my side as we head towards the enclosure gate with a further "That'll do!" in an attempt to dissuade her from darting back to the sheep. This time she reluctantly submits, her ears go back and we leave the ring to words of encouragement from Pam to both of us. In reply, Harriet streaks off to the old green bath in the corner of the field, half full of rainwater, and leaps in congratulating herself on her achievements. I fight to get my breath back and kid myself that the red cheeks are merely a glowing response to the faint praise delivered by Pam. I sink into one of the plastic garden chairs in the barn, where I satiate my thirst with coffee from Pam's flask. Never has anything tasted so good. I recount our progress to Gordon, as a dripping Harriet joins us for half my biscuit. The sheep shelter in the shade, discussing how to get the better of that ragged little dog who gets a bit big for her boots… "And she's not even a proper Collie… and her owner doesn't seem really to have got the hang of it either… Hey you over there; see if you can trip her up good and proper next time."

★ ★ ★

I smile to myself as I imagine Deborah's face if I asked her if she'd like to join me! I wonder what other leisure activity I have undertaken in my life that has been so physically exhausting. I suppose sheepherding would be called a sport and obviously when carried out at *One Man and his Dog* level it isn't as physically active… well, not for the man anyway; yes for the dog. Indeed, I remember listening to one of the country's top competitors talking about how sheepdog trialling was one of the few activities where age was no barrier; where his experience in his sixties was a bonus and his lack of physical prowess was not a disadvantage. Well, all I can say is, it's bloomin' physical right now. I can't quite believe I'm taking part in physical activity that I'm actually enjoying, having been so useless at sport all my life. I smile again as I imagine Pam saying, 'No change there then!' She clearly doesn't see me as a natural. Harriet seems to get her approval but I'm obviously seen as a non-sports person!

I learned a fear of sport at school with the humiliation of never being picked for any team until I was the only one left and some unlucky side was forced to add me to their squad, and where the ever-popular team captain struggled to place me where I would cause least harm. Memories flooded back of extremely keen pupils who behaved as though their lives depended upon winning the hockey game and who seemed to revel in running up and down in the freezing cold (in navy knickers) bashing anything that came within range of their hockey sticks. Far too frequently it seemed it was my ankles that took the force of the blows, until I learnt to hit that blasted ball to them as they thundered towards me, much to the chagrin of my own team members. I wasn't even very good at that since our school did not own such a thing as a left-handed hockey stick. Apparently I was meant to claim the ball, dash away from the marauding crowd and 'pass' it to some wing member of my team who was standing on the side-lines screaming, "To me! To me!" in true St. Trinian's fashion!

I gazed in amazement as class members flew over the 'horse' and the 'box' in the gym, my legs turning to jelly as some hefty mistress took delight in ridiculing any attempt I made to take part. I still shiver when I remember the hideousness of it.

So ingrained is the degradation of it all that my children soon learned that, while you had to be close to moribund to get a day off school, Mum was a 'soft touch' when it came to getting a letter to release you from PE (physical education).

I have a vague feeling of nausea when I pass a gymnasium or fitness training centre even now, and rapidly cross the road if I see anybody dressed for a workout session, since their ability to make rational decisions must surely be questioned.

On a lighter note, just how great is it to have a soul mate like Harriet, who has an acceptance of who I am without me trying any sort of workout? One of the greatest gifts of this relationship is that, as a woman, I don't need to worry about looking good to impress her. She won't notice if I put on a few pounds, although she has been instrumental in helping me lose a few.

I read a leaflet about 'keeping fit in retirement', only to wonder how you adapt that advice if you needed to *get* fit first. The assumption that I'd reached this milestone in a super fit state was something of a misconception on behalf of said leaflet. I arrived ready for a bus pass, never having thought about allocating time to myself to consider where I was on the fitness scale. I knew I was exhausted. I seemed to sleep almost continually for some weeks when I first retired; what bliss.

Surrounded by patients, I was able to see myself as healthy by comparison because I wasn't ill, but for me fitness was a new concept... 'getting it' primarily rather than following guidance on how to 'keep it'.

Harriet's arrival led me into maybe practising a bit of it with our walks: weight down a bit, blood pressure down without one visit to the gym, just walking, and not even at a great pace, about six miles a day. I'm sure the fitness report would say 'could do better'. After all, Harriet probably covers about three times the distance, bounding ahead and playing chase round the field with a friendly Lurcher, but then she hasn't read the retirement leaflet or given any thought to keeping fit; she hasn't asked for leg warmers or a headband yet anyway.

And now here I am, enthusiastically volunteering to run around a very often wet and muddy field, being battered and knocked over by sheep and trying to escape an over-excited dog who's not quite sure what to do with an instinct that tells her to get the sheep and bring them to me.

10

DOG WALKERS AND
DOGGIE ACTIVITIES

We met another Bearded Collie and owner this morning on our walk; a full blown show Beardie. They can never resist coming up and asking exactly what breed Harriet is, and then commiserating that she's 'not a proper Beardie'. With her tousled rough coat, the 'working Beardie' doesn't quite have the finesse of the show Bearded Collie. She looks what she is: a working breed. I drop casually into the chat that, of course historically, all Beardies looked like Harriet until breeders began to mess about with them. It could therefore be suggested that hers was the 'improper' Beardie and mine the original.

We meet the Retriever and the Labrador brigades, on the weekend walk. They circle the park, as though they are posturing for a Country Life photo shoot to demonstrate the joys of rural living; dressed in their Barbours, out with their clean, shiny dog trotting to heel with its matching collar and lead. If they let their dog off the lead sometimes maybe so many of them wouldn't be quite so fat. Dogs are such trusting creatures with so little control over their own destinies. I have a real desire to see them run free.

They nod to the couple with the Red Setter as they remove their boots and place them side by side in the special zipped Wellington boot bag in the back of the four-by-four next to their, now crated, canine.

There is a member of a relatively new breed of dog-walking-human-beings approaching as we circle round behind the football pitch. Not the first of this variety we've spotted today, the breed seems to be rapidly increasing daily. One hand is glued to the mobile phone, itself glued to the ear, with the owner of said apparatus being totally unaware of anything else going on anywhere. A lead dangles loosely from the other hand, possibly belonging to one of the dogs causing havoc somewhere over there, indeed probably this one dragging the bag from the rubbish bin, diligently distributing its contents. Could be that one that needs to be attached to that leash or maybe it's the one who has his teeth embedded in those shorts, while the footballer struggles to get free. He (or she) walking the mobile phone remains steadfastly unaware throughout.

I sometimes wonder if they get home and forget they had a dog when they started out. I'm fairly unreliably informed that it's the new way to conduct an affair: take the dog for a walk and talk to your secret lover. The level of engagement certainly makes it believable. Stories of dog-collar swapping parties are surely exaggerated?

I ruminate on the fact that it seems to be the dog owners who carry certain characteristics rather than the dogs, as I move to join the Collie ball-throwing gang in the centre of the park.

Then there's the Labradoodle contingent; he of the non-allergic variety. Supposedly, all coughs, sneezes, runny eyes and itches disappear if you buy a Labradoodle. It would seem that the whole of the south east must be afflicted with hayfever, looking at the emergent numbers of said dogs. I met Amber today, that's the owner, not the dog; she has one of these half and half Labradoodles. She tells me that Reggie is really depressed since he had his bits cut off. She hopes he will cheer up if he has a nice walk. He has a Poodle head and a Labrador body; who wouldn't be depressed? And he's probably confused as well because now he doesn't know whether he's a he or a she.

★ ★ ★

Tilly and Suvi could be forgiven for being confused. They are both special Labradoodles who are Harriet's best friends. It's our 'end-of-the-week-Friday-morning-walk-club'. Three friends chatting, three dogs playing; come rain or shine we're there. When we're all soaked to the skin, we have been known to discuss the possibility of an indoor doggie playground, where they could run and we could sit and have coffee, but most often we put the world to rights, while grumbling about the extortionate price of bread, discussing how to manage Christmas with disparate family factions coming or, on one walk of blessed memory, laughing till our sides ached commiserating with one of our party who had recently acquired three speeding tickets on one car journey taking the kids to football practice!

But yes, it is confusing for Tilly and Suvi. Both have absolutely gorgeous, woolly Labradoodle coats – one white, one black – and Harriet insists they are sheep who need to be herded around the field and definitely got out from behind that tree. In truth, should Harriet ever reach the dizzy heights of the sheepdog trial, she'll owe much of her success to the practice she's had with these two.

The blessed world of friendships is rightfully precious: loyal buddies who accept you for who you are, the good and the bad, and love you just the same are especially cherished when you live alone, helping to keep troubles in proportion, and even more special when they also love your dog.

I am privileged to have a big family of friends; many close. Tez and Val are two treasured friends who go right back to my nurse training days. We met on our first day in PTS (Preliminary Training School). Now, some fifty years later, here we are having shared the joy and grief of one another's lives, loves and children. Wherever we have been across the globe, not one of us is in any doubt of the ongoing support given freely by the other two. There is an ease between us born of our history; a family in all but blood and indeed, in many senses, we grew up together, while learning our nursing career craft, and I guess now we're growing old together.

Random memories break through when we meet up. Many of our conversations can send us into peals of laughter even now, recounting those dizzy teenage years in '60s London. Like the time we so wanted the newest craze – coloured lingerie – and, unable to afford to buy any, we boiled up our white underwear with a purple dye in the giant kettle chained to the wall at the end of the hostel corridor. Tea never tasted quite the same again made from that kettle. Then there was the time we helped Tez scale the wall to escape from the hostel – 'the virgins' retreat' as it was known – where no men, not even fathers were allowed past the front door. Tez had been summoned to Matron's office and disciplined by having her late pass cancelled for leaving a spigot (a small, rigid, plastic stopper for closing a rubber tube) in her uniform dress when it went to the laundry. We only had one late pass a month – all the way up to 10.30pm – and it was confiscated for the most minor of misdemeanours: black stocking seams not straight; and failure to strip your bed in the morning. But this time we went AWOL and we made it, out and back in, without being discovered, having spent the evening 'Rocking around the Clock' with Bill Haley, as I remember.

★ ★ ★

Harriet is rolling over and over before tearing off full pelt for a ball. The assembled group of circling dog walkers stares disapprovingly at this scruffy reprobate, as they continue their sedate weekend walk. The 'oh-dear-here-comes-that-ruffian-out-of-control-dog' fraternity reaches down and scoops their darling little fluffballs into their arms, behaving as though Harriet was about to devour Truffles whole.

I pick up the now sodden ball that has collapsed at its join making it a lopsided sphere; we slope off on foot. At least Harriet gets the chance to run off lead and knows that a walk is a daily occurrence; the great outdoors being always on offer, not a once a week display of good behaviour.

I'm heading down into the wood when an out-of-breath Dennis comes panting up the hill. He's asking if we've seen Gloria, his spaniel, who got away from him half an hour ago when she ran into the undergrowth chasing a rabbit, and hasn't returned.

The idea, when a dog goes missing, is to stand and shout like a foghorn at intervals and trust that the truant will retrace his steps at some point and find you. That will happen just as you have a vision of him streaking across the nearest road in front of a thundering lorry.

A few engrossing chats later, I'm still playing ball with Harriet when Dennis appears again still bellowing for Gloria. I note that several dogs, plus owners, begin to head for their cars and the park exits. I presume this is because many of us know for sure that even when Gloria does return (and she absolutely will, when she decides she's good and ready), she will resolutely refuse to be caught. Many an afternoon has been spent with a team of us trying to catch Gloria. As the rain begins I nevertheless feel guilty for not staying to help out Dennis, especially when I look back from the far side of the green to see his solitary figure, with cupped hands to his face, standing alone out in the middle, looking like a football ref long after the team has left the pitch.

Next time, Dennis; I promise.

★ ★ ★

There was a time when I wouldn't have had any pangs of guilt about leaving Dennis and Gloria. Those were my 'before Harriet' years.

Dogs can mark periods in one's life, boundaries between one time and another; happenings are either pre- or post-Harriet or 'we did that when Harriet was still a puppy'.

She's induced me to pay attention and to share her enthusiasm for whatever she sees. I need her to launch me into my day. The positives of the walk for me are exercise and communing with nature; a silent time of reflection. The walk for her satisfies different needs: exercise, yes, vast quantities; freedom to run unencumbered by a lead; to be reckless; to have fun with sticks; and to shout (bark) with excitement. Sniffing and pushing your nose into and around everything is of vital importance. Who's been here before? Is he friend or foe? This need to examine anywhere and everywhere with your nose is equivalent to my chat with friends at the local coffee house.

She has turned me – even me – into an outdoorsman of sorts. It is a well-known truth that no Collie owner can survive for long as a couch potato. Anything that has Collie in it doesn't just exist; it explodes with a need to keep moving and doing, bobbing and weaving, and darting under and over and around logs, trees, streams. They are astonishingly agile, which is of course why they are so good at dog agility and any other breed gets pushed into second place by them.

And there's another breed of dog-owner: the keen agility club devotee. It's great for all the dogs and they would just have a lovely time on all the equipment – up over the 'A' frame, zigzagging in and out of the weave poles, diving through the tunnels – if only their owners weren't so intense about it all. We got drummed out of the last class, Harriet and I, accused of not taking it seriously enough because I thought it was hilarious when the Border Collie, Jack, decided, on the command 'GO', to run immediately to the end of the course to claim his reward toy rather than complete the course first! Definitely not to be encouraged, Jane tells me. It's all very serious, timing is everything and Jack must learn to do it properly. Time for Harriet and me to beat a hasty exit methinks... even she seems to be aware that we're 'persona non grata' here. Harriet seems to sense things so acutely and I pick up her mood instantly, or maybe she picks up mine; I'm not sure which.

I had felt the need to do all sorts of different doggie activities with Harriet during her early years, really to use some of her excess energy and, in a way, to compensate for having only a patio and no real garden. But I then discovered that it's necessary to enjoy what it's about, to be able to truly feel part of it, and mostly we didn't! I was astonished at how fiercely competitive and deadly serious most of these turned out to be.

I loved the way Harriet would stop right at the top of the 'A' frame and balance there, looking all around, as if to say, 'Hey, look at me! I'm the King of the castle!' Apparently, I was supposed to stop this unseemly behaviour and hurry her on with a severe tone, making sure of course that she didn't fly off from halfway down the frame and that her feet touched the coloured board prior to streaking to the next bit of apparatus.

We then had a go at fly ball, where dogs run over several little jumps, grasp a tennis ball in their mouth as it shoots out from a sort of parapet in front of them, turn and run back over the jumps and drop the ball. I thought Harriet would really like this one, since it involved the much loved ball. Actually, she was scared of the noise the ball made as it was shot out of the holding equipment and it had to be simply rolled down before she was brave enough to grab it! Once again, I discovered we were into shouting and leaping about, trying to get the dog to sprint back faster and faster, with the timer and its second hand being the most significant item of tackle – certainly more important than the dog.

Then there was doggie dancing, with Harriet doing figures of eight around my legs and then weaving in and out of my legs as I walked forward. She was – well, still is – quite good at this. She will turn circles, walk on her hind legs and all sorts. The problem in the team was that she was considered untidy in the way she performed the routines; wagging her tail in the wrong places, allowing her attention to wander, and would sometimes look the other way when something caught her attention. And 'heaven forbid', she sometimes gave an excited bark in the middle of a dance routine. I was informed she was 'not a performance dog' and invited to use another dog for display purposes: a mottled Spaniel called Dougal. So we withdrew less than graciously from that game. Both Harriet and I had quite liked the dancing, and still do actually, but now we really enjoy it, performing on our own as a one man show where we and everyone else have fun.

I had a word with Harriet the day we were dismissed, somewhat unceremoniously, from the group, telling her that the failure label was meant for me, not her. I gave her an especially delicious tea of scrambled egg and cheese, making sure she understood that really she was too good for the team.

Finally, we found sheepherding – or rather it found us – and neither of us has looked back. It feels so different for her to be doing a job of work, to be engaged using her instincts, to encourage her to slow down, and to move the sheep calmly and carefully; where just she and I are working as a team, not trying to fit in with what other members want and not trying to gain approval from others. I guess I decided against doing that some time ago now.

I have a friend who, after I had Harriet, described me as a failure as a friend because I hadn't taken agility seriously and been desperate to travel with her and her dogs to agility competitions all over the country. I tried to explain to her that I was clearly in the wrong queue when competitiveness was handed out. I described how if we had gone to an agility competition together, I would have wanted her to win because it would have meant so much more to her than to me. I'm not sure she really understood what I was saying; her psyche was unable to make sense of someone who doesn't live to win.

However, she was the very friend who discovered where it might be possible for me to learn about sheepherding relatively locally. She now accuses me of being the biggest bore there is, always talking about sheepherding, and she insists on calling it sheep chasing – I have to cover Harriet's ears whenever she says it.

I guess she must have forgiven me and I further deduce that it really is 'horses for courses', or should I say 'dogs for apparatus'; mine and Harriet's apparatus being sheep. Even when 'working' at a trial, not every dog behaves as it should though. I have heard tell of a sheepdog trial where, in the middle of an outrun to collect his sheep, a Collie decided to temporarily divert from the course, dash over to a family of spectators at the edge of the course, and grab a chicken leg from their picnic before returning to complete his outrun!

Running around in my head are also thoughts about how maybe I like working alone? District nursing is a job where you are working on your own most often and, in a sense, lecturing can be quite a lonely occupation. As a district nurse, it's most often just you and your patient or family while, when lecturing, you may have a very large, raked lecture theatre, with maybe three hundred or so in the 'audience', but you are on your own at the front, doing your job alone. I go on in thought to mull over the fact that even my voluntary time with the Samaritans is on the phone; me connecting, building a relationship, one to one. This, again, might be described by many as a solitary undertaking.

Here, I am again choosing a leisure activity where I'm effectively on my own with Harriet; with a herd of sheep as my audience. Perhaps there is something in all of this that has helped, or even led me, towards leading a single life? Maybe all this is simply an acknowledgment of how uncompetitive I am.

I'm just beginning to wonder whether, in another life or time, I might have become a hermit and lived in a croft on an isolated hillside covered with sheep. I cheer myself up, remembering that my handbell ringing leisure activity is definitely not undertaken alone and I know how much I enjoy playing music as part of a team. This reassures me that I'm not on the road to becoming a complete recluse.

* * *

We're having a fantastic day here at a real live sheepdog trial. Harriet's whining enthusiastically, with stifled yelps escaping whenever the sheep come within range; she's absolutely sure that she can do a better job than the dog on the course, if only I'd let her have the chance. It's great to see how many shepherds still have difficulty controlling their dogs, even at this level with years of experience. I just want to stay here all day soaking up the atmosphere. Another time, another life, maybe I could have been here herding sheep with my very own dog...

Harriet soon gets bored with only being allowed to watch, and takes up her place lying behind the bale of hay I'm sitting on, attached to my wrist by the lead. Attached to me only because I'm not a hundred per cent sure she wouldn't dive into the field with the sheep if I gave her half a chance; so I'm just making sure. I'm quite pleased to be here today, resting her a bit, because she's got a small cut to the side of her front paw where she caught it on some barbed wire and I've dressed it with a rather neat bandage. I'm glad I haven't quite forgotten all those practical bandaging classes from preliminary training school. Sister Stedding would be quite proud of me. I didn't drop the bandage once. It's even stayed clean looking. I think Harriet might sleep for a while.

I should have been suspicious of the extended period of stillness; something that was not normally a part of Harriet's daily routine. There were those times with young children when a quiet interlude was a silent alarm that required immediate attention, but somehow the pleasure induced by the hush tended to lead to a delayed reaction; always a mistake as there was always something afoot. Afoot indeed, Harriet has removed the bandage. Evidently, the tried and tested stealthy teeth method has proved successful, her secret exposed by threads of cotton bandage hooked over a front tooth and hanging from her jaw.

★ ★ ★

11

MY RETIREMENT 'DO'

I found a new walk with Harriet today. We had circled round another footpath that I didn't know existed and, as we followed the path round the edge of the field, I was taken aback to find myself gazing over the hedge into the back garden where I had held my retirement party a few years ago.

Harriet is busy with her nose buried deep in the pile of leaves, evidently tossed over from one of the neighbouring hedges in an attempt to rid their lawn of debris. She rolls over on her back and wiggles backwards and forwards in her favourite play position, waving her legs in the air.

I turn back, to again stare at the garden. One of my sons was renting the house at the time and it was just the place I needed to enable me to invite special work friends to a leaving party.

It was still a beautiful garden now on a chilly, rather grey, winter's day, but my mind's eye immediately leaps to that warm summer evening here, with the marquee, the three piece jazz band, the laughter and the chatter.

★ ★ ★

I had carefully planned my retirement party. I so wanted those who came to be people I really wanted to be there; I had refused to have the usual leaving party given by management to supposedly 'thank' me for my past years of service. I had spent too much time, particularly in recent years, fighting management on several levels. I knew I was a 'thorn in their side' and that any 'thanks' would be false – why then would I want anyone from management at my party? But they have to come, I was told. It can't happen without, it was said. Well, it can and it did, and it gave me great pleasure to only have people there who were truly sorry to see me go.

Colleagues from various genres of my previous practice areas came. It was an exciting party that meant so much to me. Nurses, past and present, had travelled so far and given up their precious time to come and be part of it all. I'd sent invitations with a photograph of me right at the beginning of my training, dressed in what now looks like a really old-fashioned nurse's uniform: crisp white apron and butterfly cap. It's a treasured event that I'll never forget and, even now, every one of those friends who came to share it all with me has a very special place in my heart and in my memory basket. Surprisingly, the significance of the event has grown for me in the years since it happened. Rather than diminishing with time, the presence of so much care for me seems to have provided a slow motion recording in my head of it all, and I replay it often. And here I am, unbelievably, almost seeing the event again but in real time!

While it was principally a party celebrating my retirement from my district nursing post, I also invited some colleagues who had shared my lecturing life with me, which added to the vibrancy of the gathering. I had run these two parts of my career concurrently, primarily because I believed so much in the practical application of all the 'science' of nursing that I wanted to continue to practice as well as to teach. I also held fast to the principle that those of us who choose to teach the skills need to be practising them to keep the 'art' aspect of nursing alive. My teaching experience taught me that too many nursing lecturers are far removed from the practical application of all they are teaching. Indeed, a considerable number were from disciplines other than care, again accentuating the scholarly, rather than the nursing, context of the learning.

★ ★ ★

I find I can't draw my gaze away from the garden, with all the memories flooding back. I'm rooted to the spot; looking across the lawn to a small patio. The benches are still there as they had been on my party night, a little way away from the marquee, with a green climber on the wall behind. It has now reached a good bit farther up the trellis, looking strong and vital, despite now shedding its leaves. As I look across, I remember the group of medical and lecturing colleagues that had congregated there, chatting...

★ ★ ★

It was good to see these two halves together; medical and lecturing colleagues, with me being the common link. One of my lecturing colleagues described watching me manage and control three hundred students in a lecture theatre, holding their attention with stories straight from nursing practice. I'm smiling now as I remember glancing over to see one of the GPs, his hands cupped round his mouth imitating a loud hailer, shouting, "She's been managing me for years!" Everyone laughed and he went on to tell stories of joining the practice and how great it was for us to be able to discuss families together, to make joint visits, and how that working relationship benefitted patients.

I reflect now on how long it took us as district nurses to become attached to GP practices and how, previous to that, we used to work in patches, an area defined by four roads, serving anybody who lived within that 'patch' no matter who their GP was. When we became GP-attached, it meant that district nurses worked much more closely with their doctor colleagues. This GP attachment was considered a real achievement within district nursing: to be able to discuss the patient's needs directly, with feedback from both of us on progress, really targeted the continuity that families appreciated so much.

I gather this whole idea of district nurses working closely with the GP is well on the way out now. The GP used to meet with the district nurse attached to his surgery to discuss and hand over details on any patient he wanted his district nurse to see. He now has to make a referral for care to a central point; to an administrator for triaging. The administrator will then divert that visit anywhere, to any community nurse who has a list of visits on the computer that shows she has minutes to spare today, i.e. dependency code deficit! Unfortunately, there is no code that accounts for the patient who may need more time today than just the giving of her injection, and who may really want to see the same nurse; the one he knows and trusts.

I remember the speeches going on well into the night with colleagues. The doctors I had worked with talking about patients we had visited together – touching stories; humorous stories.

Even as I listened then to kind comments on my personal commitment to patient care, I had a very strong sense that what was happening here was not only a goodbye to me, but rather a goodbye to an era. This celebration was somehow farewell to a time in nursing that had almost disappeared, to a time when it was apposite to consider nursing a vocation – when to talk of 'serving' was not a cause for sniggering laughter and when the oft hidden art of care was acknowledged alongside the science, both being equally valued.

There was a time when students came into the profession driven by a desire to become experts in this art of caring, rather than how they enter now, with aspirations of impersonating the doctor by running around with intravenous drugs in a kidney dish, feeling important.

When did it change? I suspect it was when nursing *management* took precedence over those undertaking 'hands-on' care and when it was deemed that the apprenticeship model of learning this caring art was unsatisfactory and that a degree was necessary to nurse.

To some extent, we, as a profession, have ourselves to blame for the swing to university education being adopted as the way forward. Nurses began to rebel against the vocational aspect of nursing; the way of describing it as 'a calling'. This became not just unfashionable but something to rise up and challenge, and it went alongside nurses shouting loudly about poor pay. There was a constant push for payment for unsocial hours and the battle was won with night duties and weekend shifts reaping increased financial rewards. I never empathised with this wave of discontent, believing we had entered the profession knowing it was a twenty-four hour, seven day a week job, so I never understood why working any of those hours was deserving of more money. No-one who longed for a nine-to-five job would ever have considered nursing.

What followed this was the reduction of staff numbers rostered at the duty times that demanded higher rates of pay, with fewer members of staff to undertake the same levels of care at unsocial hours. Patients are ill as frequently at weekends and nights as during the nine-to-five weekday hours, but they are served by fewer, less qualified (and therefore cheaper) staff members. This did not happen prior to this change in pay scales. Of course, there were societal changes elsewhere across the board, but nursing had previously always been considered a separate case; one that didn't conform to changes that would disadvantage patients. As I remember it, this was the point when there was a change in attitudes.

What seemed to follow on from this somewhat militant demand for more money was an undercurrent of 'we're worth more than this' and 'what we do is sufficiently important for us to get a degree'! Again, there was a push for many more people to complete a degree – in almost anything it would seem – with very little consideration given as to whether or not it was always the best way to learn a particular craft. The tables began to turn. Nursing students were to become academic students attending university to learn what was fundamentally a practical skill: caring for the sick.

I don't think anyone in the profession would deny the need for higher education further up the career ladder, but a growing number of nurses are beginning to question whether this is the best, the most successful, way to learn how to care for the vulnerable members among us.

Shortly before I retired, I had a student nurse allocated to my area of practice for two weeks to attend patients with me, to observe district nursing work. We visited several dying patients and their families. At the end of the first day, I was really taken aback when she asked, "Which course is it I need to go on to learn how to talk to people like you do?" We went on to talk about how getting an A for her latest essay on communication skills had failed her because she felt unprepared to 'talk to people who were upset'.

I wonder if those nurses who pushed so hard for what we've got now have ever considered that the old adage about 'being careful what you wish for' might have a real ring of truth about it in this instance.

★ ★ ★

I look across at the large Magnolia tree in the far corner, with its garden seat and table. There are no Magnolia blooms now and, even at my party, the tree had finished flowering; but the canopy formed by the leaves was thicker and the green of the leaves more vivid. It is a magnificent tree with a mock streetlamp standing tall at the far end.

★ ★ ★

It was here, under this tree, when the last guest had left, that I had sat and read the many cards that had been sent or brought with the many presents that adorned the table. My four children were busy clearing the remains of the party, while I sat with a last glass of wine and read each card with its cherished words.

The first card had a picture of a large mother bird on a branch hovering over her nest of fledglings. The speech bubble from her beak said, 'Goodbye and Good Luck!' As I opened it up, the handwriting said 'I'm a better nurse because of you'. It was signed by Maria.

I had taught Maria during her training. She was a keen student and I was really pleased that she had attained the post she wanted.

Maria was one of the trainees I taught when I went into nurse education, after it moved from the old 'hospital school of nursing' model of training into the university.

Following this decision, the whole focus of training changed. The emphasis now was getting the students through their degree programmes with more time spent in 'school' and less time on the ward, thus accentuating their academic student status, rather than highlighting the real learning to be absorbed by 'doing' as a junior member of the workforce.

I took the position of senior lecturer because I believed we had to redress the balance and, I suspect, I believed I could inspire nurse trainees with a desire to care, and so encourage the art alongside the science with stories and more stories of 'care in action'.

I summon up Maria in my mind: she was one of about fifty students who had come to learn about pain management for dying patients. I recall how they had all come with pens and notebooks poised ready to list the necessary drug names, dosages, and side effects. I remember the session well. The quizzical faces indicated that they were startled to learn that it wasn't all just about the where, when and how of drug regimens but, more importantly, it needed their ability to 'be with' their patient, to listen to the meaning of the moment for them, and to validate their pain experience; to reassure and to comfort them.

Again, standing here today I feel I am watching a replay of my retirement party. I remember that Maria had come to me after this lecture and told me she'd learned something special that day: she'd learned what the essence of nursing was all about, she said. I was touched by her words.

I laugh now as I glance over to the tree and recollect the warm evening and the light from the lamp as it fell across Maria's card. At the bottom of the card she quoted me:

> *'Pain is a huge experience that cannot be sorted out by just the giving of an analgesic!'*

★ ★ ★

Thank you, Maria, for giving me this feedback. Maybe my voice was not always crying in the wilderness.

Maria's card and comments made me think of my conversation with the Dean at my exit interview before I retired. She asked if I could offer any reason why I had such a consistently high attendance record from the students (there is no compulsory attendance required as a university trainee nurse student!). I responded, saying that on the feedback sheets that the students submitted, there were always comments about how great it was to have real life stories from someone working out in practice to make the learning live.

It seems as though the students themselves are asking for more 'hands-on' learning. They themselves are perhaps feeling that their placements into different areas of practice are not giving them sufficient experience to maximise their learning; to match the theory to practice and put it all together.

★ ★ ★

The picture of the garden stayed vividly with me as I returned to my walk. The sound of happy voices, the jazz band playing, the clatter of cutlery on plates amidst sudden shrieks of laughter, seemed graphically there in my head. I could feel the cards and letters in my hands and I remember putting them away later with other letters I had received from patients and relatives.

★ ★ ★

I had kept them all and, as I walked, I sifted through them in my thoughts. Many of the letters were from family members thanking me for the care I had given to a loved one…

A grateful son thanked me for the many conversations I had had with his ninety-year-old mother, Martha, with her sharing her feelings about wanting to die now. Her immobility and loss of independence had become huge burdens for her and she explained what a relief it was to be able to talk about it to me; her innermost thoughts being too painful to discuss with family. This somehow enabled her to manage a little longer, knowing that the opportunity was there to offload with someone who was 'her nurse; a professional who offered her the understanding and the confidentiality she wanted'. I knew there would be no support offered to other Marthas now. There would be no allocation of time by a district nurse to the increasing number of Marthas in our community anymore.

She wouldn't justify a visit now; after all, what 'nursing need' could be applied to her affliction? What dreaded dependency code could be allocated?

Like pages fluttering over in a book, more cards and letters flashed in front of my mind's eye. My thoughts then rested on a rather scrappy piece of paper with only a few words on it.

GEORGIE

Georgie was only forty-two years old when she died, in her bed by the window, looking out on to the garden she loved so much. Her cancer-ravaged body was painfully thin with sallow skin stretched over bony prominences, while her abdomen was incongruously distended with fluid. Any movement was exhausting for her.

I thought back to an earlier time with Georgie. She was stronger then and treatment was continuing. But the outlook for Georgie was never good even then: the tumour had metastasised and spread. She was undergoing heavy chemotherapy with a less than twenty per cent chance of survival. But she felt she was strong; she was going to be one who would make it.

As she began to deteriorate, I knew that she knew things were not working, that she was not recovering as she expected and that her condition was worsening. I remember feeling decidedly angry for Georgie who had fought so hard; angry because I had never understood why cancer was the only disease I knew of where people were expected to *fight*. What was this insistence on *fighting* cancer that left patients like Georgie feeling that if treatment failed it was their fault because somehow they hadn't fought hard enough or long enough? Georgie had indeed fought; there was nothing defeatist about her attitude.

We began picking up the pieces and talking about Georgie's limited prognosis, when she really knew all hope was gone.

"They as good as promised me an extra year or two if I agreed to more treatment; to more chemo." Georgie's voice was loud and strident. "What the bloody hell was all that for? It's given me sod all!"

She had felt shocked on being told nothing more could be done. She'd hated the suspense, always wondering when the bad news might come. Now the suspense was over; Georgie hit a low point, but not for long. She very soon seemed to become more talkative than I'd known her while she was undergoing therapy – almost more lively in the face of the failed chemotherapy. We talked about how now that she didn't have hope anymore, it was the end of living in a limbo of hope.

"I'm sick of always wondering what's going to come to light each time I go for another appointment," she said. "I don't have to wonder any more… it's here. Why do people keep saying 'never give up hope' as though hope was something solid, something to cling to?" She asked the question, never expecting a reply. It hung in the air between us…

She had felt it hovering around for so long, through one course of chemo after another, tempting her all the time. Georgie taught me a lot about the support needed, before and after, those continual appointments and the changing hope trajectory that accompanied each of them.

Now hope had disappeared, Georgie felt almost more cheerful. It seemed it had been the hope, the suspense, that had been so hard to endure and so exhausting. We could now talk about the things she wanted to achieve in the time she had left and how we could work together to make them happen. Two close friends had taken part in Georgie's wish list, helping her to visit some gardens she'd always wanted to see. They had worked lovingly on her garden at home so that by the time she could no longer make the stairs, she could see some beautiful displays of flowers from her bed which we positioned in front of the French windows. She made her own wish list – 'Things to do before I die' – and gradually we made them happen and ticked them off one by one. It even included a Chinese meal with four friends one evening around her bed about a week before she died. I made an evening visit to be sure the pain was under control before the friends arrived. It was a good evening; a treasured time for both Georgie and her friends.

The last wish on her list was that after she died I would dress her in a particular nightdress and make sure her face was made up as she liked. She wanted to look good when she met her maker, she told me. I'd had several practices beforehand, until she was satisfied with my handiwork.

On the night Georgie died, she had on her chosen lipstick. I went to the drawer to get the nightie. On the top, lay a little crumpled note. The writing was shaky. I could hear her voice as I read:

'You didn't give me any more days in my life, but you did put life into my days… thanks'

I can feel the tears pricking in my eyes now as I recall the note, and push my hand deep into my pocket as if to secrete the note there. I'm thinking hard, swiftly searching for an answer as to who would do that for other Georgies now? What would be the dependency code for that extra care... the going-the-extra-mile care? It's doubtful this would come under the heading of a 'nursing need'.

Patients now have to prove they have a 'nursing need' before the district nurse can take them on to the caseload. What constitutes a 'nursing need' causes considerable debate in management hierarchy. Being unable to manage your own toileting requirements does *not* constitute a nursing need. This absurd argument about what is nursing care and what is social care groans on continually. It's all about budgets. If we can say there is no 'nursing need', then the health budget is safe and we can make sure that the social service pot pays for it and, of course, patients then have to contribute if we say it's nothing to do with *health*. Needing help to get to the toilet or help getting up, getting dressed or getting to bed are now definitely not 'nursing needs' – they're now categorised as 'social care'.

It seems that now referral to another service is the name of the game. If social services, intermediate care, rapid response or continuing care (to name but a few) can be persuaded to attend, then whoopee do! If that can't be made to happen then the district nurse may reluctantly visit and hopefully find time to allocate the dependency code. Does anyone but a member of management want to know what a dependency code is...?

Dependency codes allocate a certain amount of time to each visit once the 'nursing need' has been established – an injection would probably be fifteen minutes and a code 'A', while a large wound dressing would be given thirty minutes and a code 'B'.

The dependency code is supposed to allow management to make sure each nurse is making a sufficient number of 'appropriate' visits and to equalise work across a corporate caseload. This means no nurse has her own caseload anymore; her work list is picked up from the computer. It will have been allocated by a non-nurse; so, someone who allocates as per dependency code, not by patient need. This means much less continuity of care for the patient. Allocation will be according to which nurse has spare code minutes available... and, of course, all to be triaged – but don't let's start with that bit of gobbledygook!

Even as I say it now, out loud with only Harriet to listen, I wonder how many of those jargon phrases would have meant anything to Martha. The sort of support Martha needed to prevent her sinking into depression, or the support that could enable a long-suffering daughter caring for an elderly mother with dementia to cope, is not classified as a 'nursing need' and therefore doesn't rate a dependency code.

★ ★ ★

My head is dizzy with the thoughts of the ridiculousness of all that management speak. As I step it out across the field, heading for the wood, I feel anger rising in my chest.

★ ★ ★

These were the buzz words that meant nothing but got in the way of care; just care, that's all we want, answering a patient's needs rather than management's. And yet we're now teaching our nurses that it's management that has to be served. The patient is secondary, well behind the needs of management and even further down the list really because feeding the computer with data has to take first priority.

What is the meaning of the verb 'to nurse'? Not what is 'a nurse' but what meaning is held within the verb? What does the task of 'nursing' entail? Implicit within that 'doing', is taking care of; looking after. This is our fundamental purpose. The intention of all who call themselves nurses *is* to nurse; what we do is defined by and displayed in our job title. This caring for, this nurturing, has compassion at its heart.

My mind raced on to the care and compassion patients who died at home needed, and how often it was the listening, the being available, the making conversations possible between them and their families that made sense of what was happening, and so put meaning into last days. To be able to move a conspiracy of silence forward, to allow families to share their sadness, offers opportunities for all parties to really make the most of precious time together, to recognise the importance of endings that allow the surviving partner or family to say their goodbyes and to cope with their grief. These were healing moments, immeasurable in value… but without a dependency code.

Over time, where previously certain nursing treatments were only carried out in hospital, increased technical skill has been needed by district nurses to undertake these tasks at home. Many times, such techniques and changes have improved the care available to patients at home. In the '60s and '70s, patients who were dying in pain needed injections of morphine regularly. It was sometimes almost impossible to time visits and get back on the bike making sure the patient wasn't in acute pain while waiting for the next injection. Now, together with the huge strides that have been made in our understanding and administration of analgesic drug regimens, pain management in the community has rapidly improved. We have devices that allow continuous administration of necessary drugs, enabling the patient to remain pain-free for many hours.

These tasks would certainly be said to be a 'nursing need' and, therefore, can be allocated a code, but it is indisputably only part of what constitutes nursing care. If we continue to suggest that nurses should only operate at this advanced task level and we take the general caring tasks away from what they do, then we accentuate the impression that these technical tasks are what constitute nursing care. In so doing, we diminish and devalue the significance of the general, the *essential,* nursing care that we have now, in so many instances, taken away from nurses and allocated to social service carers.

What are these essential nursing care tasks that we have given away to the social service department; indicating that they are no longer considered to be part of *health* concerns? This is the care that we know is highly valued by patients. Personal care tasks such as helping patients with toileting needs and bathing were, historically, tasks carried out by nurses. They were where we learnt about caring with dignity; where we learnt about talking to patients, finding out how they were feeling, and what was really concerning them right then. It is this sharing, when patients are at their most vulnerable, that teaches us our compassion. During this personal care patients reveal their innermost concerns and fears with us, teaching us the value of this nursing art, allowing us to match it to our technical science abilities.

To deprive nurses of these valuable learning opportunities – engaging with patients at their most vulnerable and most dependent – robs them of soaking up the very essence of care, the core concepts of nursing, just by absorbing it through their skin. Add to this the emphasis now placed on the degree curriculum and learning to reference correctly we shouldn't be surprised that the profession is now discussing how we can select people for nursing who are compassionate and who understand the meaning of dignity? How very sad all this is, when it's all there, with every patient ready to show us how to supply all those vital skills that are so important to patients but almost impossible to measure.

I believe it was Einstein who said,

'Experience is knowledge. All else is information.'

Who has decided that what is measurable is good? If it can't be measured, documented, made into figures for management, then the care task is considered to be without value and… thus unworthy of a dependency code.

This approach developed when the profession concluded that

to manage nurses, to move away from 'hands-on' nursing, was a really important job that could realise monetary rewards way beyond those afforded to their uniformed brethren. So, stepping into management, rather than delivering direct patient care, became the name of the game, with all its attention on figures and statistics, with bonuses being awarded for 'saving money'. That translated into a reduction in the practical workforce that of course released funds... probably for more managers.

Was I just refusing to accept that change happens, that change is good? I think back to my view of the garden just now and the climber I had noted on the wall by the French windows. It looked much taller than a few years ago at my party. Change happens: things grow and develop. I remember how it looks, top heavy now, almost as though it has outgrown its strength. The bed it is planted in, between the patio slabs and the wall, is too narrow for the root system to extend sufficiently to support the increasing foliage above. It's struggling and needs some really good mulch and TLC to enable it to survive. Would district nursing survive, or would management targets continue to choke and threaten its very existence, let alone the quality of care it provides?

★ ★ ★

Harriet is quite a way ahead of me as we enter the wood and I feel a sudden chill as I tighten my scarf around my neck and zip my jacket right up. My pace is now slow and laboured as I try to adjust to an ache in the pit of my stomach prompted by this deliberation.

I try hard to pull my mind away from my garden view.

★ ★ ★

I felt a warm glow as I remembered the event, but was aware of a bitter sweetness amongst the memories; a realisation that this heavy feeling of sadness was here to stay. We have lost touch with a better time in nursing: a time never to return. It feels like a bereavement; like a wave of grief sweeping aside the joyfulness when I'd first glimpsed the garden with its loaded memories of the party.

Grief and fear are the closest of bedfellows; am I grieving the loss of this valuable healing art or fearful for a world that doesn't even recognise what has gone?

Increasingly, I'd felt I was struggling to hold the sea back from covering England and I'd failed abysmally. The tide of management wants, instead of patients' needs, continues to rush in and is continually beating against the cliff of care, wearing it away, until finally whole areas crumble to be reclaimed by the sea. We all then just stay away from the edge; we don't get too close, we don't even look over, so that we don't have to admit what's happening. We don't then have to see the whole chunks of cliff that have been worn away. Are we failing right now to recognise the real care that's missing, that's being eroded away under our noses?

It seems that, with the rise in technology, we've dismissed the basic nursing truth that sensitive nursing care does make a difference. Therapeutic relationships in nursing make patients feel better; these relationships are built when patients are at their most vulnerable.

"When a nurse encounters another, something happens.
What occurs is never a neutral event.
A pulse taken, words exchanged, a touch, a healing moment…
Two persons are never the same."

(Dossey, Keegan, Guzzetta and Kolkmeier 1995)

12

HERDING, HOLIDAYS AND HEARSAY

We're having a really good walk today around some beautiful countryside in Lancashire. I've spread my wings and come up here for another sheepherding holiday. Absolutely blissful: Harriet and I with a field of sheep to ourselves for a week – my favourite sheep too, Herdwicks, so we can practise all we've learnt several times a day with some instruction in the morning to help us along and put us right. To be fair, it's mostly me who's being instructed; apparently I'm not listening to (watching) the signals Harriet is giving me. I'm also reminded that Harriet can read what the sheep are doing better than I ever will and that if I learn to read her signals better, I'll be in a position to help her carry out what I'm wanting her to do: to get her to interpret the signals and whistles I'm giving her.

I can't quite believe I'm here now, identifying Herdwick sheep, when, just a couple of years ago, if you'd asked me anything about sheep, I would have supposed they were all either white or sometimes black with lots of wool all over and a leg at each corner.

It also occurs to me, as we walk along a high ridge looking down over the green valley with sheep everywhere, that if I were to reflect now on any regrets in my life, there may be sadness that I haven't managed to own a field with my own sheep – hardly likely to become reality for someone whose finances run to owning a one-bedroom flat with a postage stamp patio that just manages to include one garden chair! However, I ruminate on how this week of sheepherding is a wonderful second best to owning a field of sheep of my own and how wonderful a cup of coffee tastes sitting on my patio on a

very early sunny spring morning. We stride on together, Harriet with her
nose sniffing everything, only breaking off every now and then to roll over on
her back and jiggle about.

★ ★ ★

I admonish myself for ever thinking I want more than I've already
got in life, and I hear one of my mum's phrases resounding in my
head…

"Don't want what you can be happy with but rather learn to be
happy with what you've got."

But even as I hear that, I find my mind playing with the idea of
how my life might have been different had I gone into
sheepherding at an early age and eventually got as far as owning
and working my own sheep. Strangely, the more we do it the more
the everyday farming-type tasks I do with Harriet bring me great
feelings of achievement and satisfaction.

Somehow 'peaks' of teaching Harriet to bring the sheep into
the pen or to herd them down the run, maybe to get them out of a
tricky corner, all seem to take precedence for me over any ideas of
competing in sheepdog trials. I seem to just want her to be a good
farm dog.

It's almost as though the unclimbed peak where I might want
to plant my flag has changed over the time I've got involved in this
hobby. Even more extraordinary, it doesn't seem right to call it a
hobby anymore – which is ridiculous because that is exactly what
it is – but it's as though I want it to be Harriet's and my job of
work.

These thoughts all assembled together in my head after I
overheard a comment from my kids. They had accompanied me
on my sheepherding holiday; all going off doing their own thing in
the surrounding area. They went walking, biking, visiting local
towns, and the rest, while Harriet and I worked our sheep. It was
great to be with them and to share lovely meals together in the

farmhouse-like kitchen. Even more so since they did most of the cooking and are somewhat more accomplished in the culinary department than I am. To listen to them bantering with one another, laughing at all the 'in' family jokes, and all enjoying their break from their various employments, was reminiscent of Christmas gatherings and I am reminded again of how lucky I am to have them with me.

I had just left them all in the barn lounge as I called Harriet and announced we were going up to our allotted field of sheep to have another session. As I was putting on my boots outside the door, I heard one of them saying:

"Did either of you know Mum harboured these latent aspirations to be involved with all this countryside sheep stuff?"

Amid peals of laughter came the immediate response in chorus: "No!"

No, I didn't know either, I thought, and I grinned to myself as Harriet and I walked off up the drive to our sheep. I have got fantastic kids who not only come on this sort of holiday with me but who have, together, bought it for me for a birthday present. How thoughtful and generous is that? Particularly when I recall how Izzie, when she moved to a new job recently, resolutely refused to look at anything to rent that wasn't within easy reach of an all-night supermarket! I think, perhaps, they may all be city dwellers at heart, and yet here they are, with me, way out in the countryside.

We're staying in a beautifully converted, five-star, self-catering barn on a sheep farm in Lancashire. It's turning out to be my ideal holiday. I've never been a 'laying-on-the-beach-going-golden-brown' girl myself, primarily because I burn and freckle as soon as the sun shows itself and I seem to have spent most good summers smothered in factor fifty sun cream and hiding in the shade. Here, still with the factor fifty, over a warm Easter, Harriet and I have been given a field of our own for the week... a field with its own sheep that we can pretend are ours and visit as many times a day as we choose, practising the skills we're struggling to learn. We're being helped by a sheepdog trainer of considerable note and I feel privileged that he's been prepared to give us his time and patience, let alone loan us his sheep. I'm not sure Harriet considers it a privilege. She shot him a look this morning that said, "Who are you in my field? Just move aside and let me get to the sheep." It was amazing to see how quickly she reacted to his presence though and how soon she realised that here was someone who really did know what he was doing and who could read the sheep as well as her… well, nearly anyway. She seemed to be thinking "Hello… p'raps I'd better listen here. 'He who must be obeyed' has spoken." I'm sure she went on to hope he could teach me something too. Indeed, I swear that snort as she shook her head was a disguised laugh as she heard him telling me: "Let her go. She can do it. Have confidence in her."

I'm loving the whole feel of the farm life. While country life has moved on from the village life I experienced as a child, there is still a feeling of space, and somehow the seasons appear to hold more meaning for those who live here than they do for city folks. Their lives have an altered base. We're just past the bulk of lambing here, with all its sense of spring and new beginnings, and with it the suggestion of long hours and hard work that it entails. It's as though the vital points of reference here in the countryside are distinctly different from those in the more materially founded urban areas of home. Maybe it's a harder life than we part-time visitors understand. I look at the collection of Border Collie dogs living at the farm. They are kennelled outside in all weathers and they all bark as we pass. Well cared for yes, but they're appreciated as working dogs; not pets. Not for them central heating, a warm soft bed or marmite crusts for tea. It's a sense not exactly of hardship that's reflected in the community life around, more a sense of reality juxtaposed with these seasons; maybe it's the struggle with the elements and an existence with less control over what life chooses to deliver. There's a truth here, where, in some ways, fortitude and resilience replace sentimentality.

Well, I think we both came back with more confidence and a determination to return; to look out again at the views, rolling hills covered with sheep and gambolling lambs. Harriet curls up on the sofa next to me, as I wonder how much progress we can make before we return. "Maybe I can get you fully onto the whistle by then," I murmur. "Maybe we could even manage to pen some sheep. Last time we tried that I seem to remember you thought you'd drive *me* into the pen and leave the sheep circling outside. What was it our trainer said? 'Well, Rome wasn't built in a day'!"

★ ★ ★

Both Harriet and I definitely need our confidence this morning. We're back home but have been given an opportunity to work two-hundred sheep in a sixty-acre field just a few miles away.

I'm still on an absolute high and can't quite come down from those giddy heights: sending Harriet way out on an outrun, probably the longest she's managed. It wasn't perfect but it wasn't too bad either. She didn't plough through the middle, which I dreaded she might, and she didn't cross in front of them either. She went round on the flank I gave her, gathered all two-hundred sheep and brought them down the field to me... somewhat faster than she should, but she did it. While she went down the hefty bank with them, out of view, about five-hundred yards from me, my heart was in my mouth waiting for the sheep to come up into view. Where were the sheep? Where was Harriet? Then, slowly, (it was quite a steep hill) a long row of little white heads bobbed above the eye-line, followed by sheep and more sheep, and behind them all was my very own sheepdog flanking from right to left keeping them together. It's a picture in my mind that I'll hold onto forever. I gave her a stop command as the sheep came frighteningly fast towards me. This allowed the sheep to settle down somewhat, while I flanked her to her left and tried to get her to walk them across in front of me; all the while, I struggled to read the signals she was giving me about the sheep and where they were heading.

My heart rate settles along with those of the sheep. There was a scary moment there when a headstone loomed large in my mind's eye with 'trampled to death by eight-hundred cloven hooves' written across it.

I call her off with a "That'll do" and stroke her gently on her head, as she lifts her nose up to look at me, clearly pleased with herself. I know she's saying, "Didn't I do well?" Both she and I are on cloud nine, unable to believe we've done it together. We're both exhausted too and she has good reason for that; she's run a long way. My tiredness is the result of recovering from the excitement.

Inwardly, I thank her for showing me how to help her carry out the whole manoeuvre. As we walk to the gate, I reflect on the fact that, yes, it is indeed her teaching me, and I begin to think how often patients themselves were my teachers…

★ ★ ★

MARGUERITE

When I had first visited Marguerite, her gruesome diagnosis had been immediately obvious. After struggling to open the door to me, using both her hands to exert the pull she needed, her head was bowed down onto her chest, eyes on the floor and she had then placed both hands firmly on her forehead and pushed her head up to see who I was. I had been asked by the GP to visit this sixty-year-old lady as soon as possible as she had recently been told she had motor neurone disease (MND).

This life-limiting, progressive, degenerative disease leads to weakness and wasting of muscles, causing increasing lack of mobility in the limbs, and difficulties with speech, swallowing and breathing. There is currently no treatment that will halt the progress of the disease. The body continues to become weaker, while the intellect remains unaffected. In Marguerite's case, her neck muscles were affected as one of the early presenting signs of the disease… somewhat unusually in my experience.

Within a very few weeks, Marguerite could only shuffle slowly with help, from bed to chair, where Charlie, her beloved cat, sat waiting for her to be positioned. She was unable to speak, using her right thumb up or down to signify yes or no, while her flaccid, lifeless arm was supported along one arm of the chair. Now, she was unable to hold her head up at all and I would position a folded scarf across her forehead and secure it around the headrest of her chair.

Opposite her chair, on the other side of the fireplace, was another chair; an all-singing-all-dancing chair that would go up and down, back and forwards, at the touch of a button. On said chair lay a metal back brace, to which was attached a neck stem with a halo band attached to its upper end. This was some of the equipment provided by the physiotherapist. Marguerite was supposed to wear and use these daily but she steadfastly refused. She hated the halo contraption that was intended to grip and support her head. We 'discussed' my concerns that, should my improvised scarf head support fail, there was a danger of her head falling very heavily forward, carrying with it the very real possibility of breaking her neck. Marguerite chose to accept this risk and held fast to her decision.

She could manage to stroke Charlie as he had learned to sit on the arm of her old chair within reach of her one thumb and the arms of the clever chair weren't wide enough for him. We both came to dread the well-intentioned visits from the physiotherapist who kept writing notes admonishing us both for not using her apparatus.

I obtained an adapted word processor, a 'lite' writer, through the speech therapy department, that would have enabled Marguerite to punch messages on to a screen with her thumb. She dismissed this too. I managed to develop a way of communicating using a tin tray and children's magnetic alphabet letters that Marguerite could just move with her one thumb. It was then I discovered that she had been an extremely able, high-speed typist prior to her illness, and found the laborious typing on the word processor just too awful, reminding her constantly of the abilities she had lost. She shared with me, using the letters on the tin tray, the mental anguish it caused her. From then on this was the way we communicated, the way we shared our thoughts, and I learned what was important to Marguerite. It was hardly high tech but it worked.

As I dried her tears, I mopped the incessant drool that escaped from Marguerite's mouth. As the muscle weakness intensified, it became increasingly difficult for her to even swallow her own saliva. This intelligent lady, trapped in a failing body, struggled to make some sense of what was happening to her and, to the end, fought to make her own decisions. I got to know her well over the months of her illness and, while it often presented us with problems, I think Marguerite's refusal to conform was something I admired about her. I missed 'talking' with her on our tin tray when she died.

In one of the last 'tin tray conversations' I had with Marguerite, I had asked her what things we, the district nurses, had done for her over these months that she felt had helped her and what else she would have liked us to have done. Laboriously, she moved the childish letters. Finally the message read:

'You nursed me, not my disease…'

Our patients are our teachers only if we take the time to listen to them; and only if we really listen, rather than half listen while actually planning what we want to say next.

Even as I'm thinking about Marguerite and how much there is to learn from what patients say to us, my thoughts gallop forward to a time when the learning I needed came by way of a patient's actions, rather than her words.

PHYLLIS

The Matron of our local cottage hospital (I believe 'lead nurse' is the term used now) had asked to see me about a patient they had who wanted to be discharged home and thus would then have been under my care. So often these small local cottage hospitals were loved and prized by patients who had great attachment and loyalty to 'their hospital', where the standard of nursing care was often second to none and where there was continuity of care between hospital and community staff. They also enabled relatives to visit easily, easing the fear and loneliness of illness and disease. They were serviced by the local GPs and therefore hospital and community staff frequently worked closely together delivering care to the surrounding locality.

These centres of excellence are almost non-existent now; closed down by health authorities who have as their mantra 'bigger must be better' and who seem to be able to convince themselves that patients need to travel as far away as possible from their homes when they need an operation. They appear to believe that patients are so desirous of change that they want to go to a town and surgical team they've never heard of, where relatives can't afford either the time or the hospital parking fees to visit, and where public transport is infrequent and inconvenient.

I went into Matron's office at lunchtime and we had a cup of coffee while she talked to me about Phyllis. Phyllis had been admitted by ambulance some three weeks earlier, unconscious and generally in a very poor state of health, having fallen down the stone steps in her back garden. Apart from her head wound, Phyllis had a large, macerated area on her right buttock, where a neglected cancerous tumour from the lower bowel had broken through and was now just an infected, ulcerating cavity involving most of the buttock tissue. Phyllis had arrived on the ward with several old towels covering the area and held in place by her knickers.

Matron went on to explain that the ambulance men felt that her home was not fit to discharge Phyllis to. The house was in a very dilapidated state with many broken windows, only one (cold) tap in use, and with no heat or light due to the electricity having been cut off because of non-payment of bills. There had also been a water leak at some time that had rotted several of the stair treads, leaving no access to the upstairs. Phyllis had been living in the sitting room and sleeping on the sofa for a long time.

I gathered that Phyllis was causing considerable havoc while on the ward, with her continual loud insistence that she wanted to go home. She was an alcoholic and, whilst she really wanted the pain medication she was receiving in hospital, she also wanted alcohol and had become quite challenging during her stay.

"I've got to get back to feed my cat," she told me.

I made a pact with Phyllis that if she would stay in hospital until I could get a couple of windows mended and the electricity turned back on, I would see the cat was fed, and she could then come home if she still wanted to. Eventually, her neighbours reluctantly agreed to feed the cat, although they admitted to being somewhat fed up with Phyllis throwing her empty bottles over the fence during her drunken episodes.

With the help of a few charitable bodies, we were able to get light and heat, making Phyllis's room suitable for her to come home to. I'd actually even managed, with considerable difficulty, to arrange for a hospital bed to be erected in her room, to avoid her having to sleep on the old, somewhat damp sofa.

Phyllis was fully aware that the cancer couldn't be cured and that her life expectancy was very limited, and we talked about the possibility of sudden haemorrhage and of her dying at home alone. She said she knew that would happen but stated that if she wanted to go home to die and not to stay in hospital then it was her choice and we should stop interfering. She was right. What authority had we to judge how she should live? Or die? Phyllis was discharged home, agreeing to daily visits from the district nurses to dress her tumour wounds.

It was raining the following day when I made my visit. As I pulled up outside the house, there, on the front path, was my precious hospital bed, complete with a very sodden mattress covered in puddles.

"If I'd wanted a proper bed, I'd uv asked for one. Since *you* wanted the bed, *you* can bloomin' well 'av' it. Take it away with you!" Phyllis said.

Phyllis's husband had died several years previously and listening to her talk about him, it was obvious that her drinking had, in her words, 'got out of hand after he went'. She still missed him dreadfully and would play Victor Sylvester records on her battered old record player, remembering the times they had danced to those tunes together.

She did die alone, on her old sofa as she'd wanted, and I learned to think again before deciding what I felt was best for patients, and maybe to hesitate and consider who it was for, who really wanted or needed it, before I made my decisions.

★ ★ ★

We're out on an early evening walk. It's not too cold, although we had a warmer spell in March than it's managing to give us now at the end of April. We've found another footpath that we're busy investigating and we've come across a small field of ewes with their lambs. I can't resist stopping to watch. There's a timeless feeling of lambs and spring, rather like the ebb and flow of the tide; whatever may befall us, these simple joys will always be here, year in and year out. The distant sound of church bells calling the community to church and evensong somehow authenticates the rural scene.

★ ★ ★

As I'm leaning on the fence watching this display of gambolling lambs and peacefully grazing ewes, listening to the bell peals, I find myself smiling as I remember last week's handbell ringing practise; in itself, a sort of country pursuit I suppose. While it's not extinct within town communities, I've always suspected that there are more small handbell ringing groups in country villages; like the one I belong to. Indeed, we have a local bell festival each year, where several handbell ringing groups from several surrounding parishes meet and play for one another; always a fun occasion, with lots of chat and sharing of ideas and music. I've been a handbell ringer for quite a number of years and am still taken aback by how special it is to make music together. I've often wished Mum had lived to hear me play bells; her talent for playing the piano had not been inherited by either her daughters or her grandchildren and she so loved her music. I think she might have loved mine too.

At our recent practice I just couldn't resist smiling as we turned to the first piece of music and prepared to play...

'Sheep may Safely Graze' was there; displayed in all its glory.

Not while Harriet's around, I thought.

Could we, Harriet and I, one day gather all those grazing ewes with such a good outrun, such a steady considered lift and fetch, that even Handel might approve?

★ ★ ★

We've come out early this morning for our walk. We're early because it's the first day of our long weekend in Cornwall. Harriet and I now stand up on the edge of the sand dunes as they creep up the craggy bank, just before the terrain becomes rougher, the grass tougher and well-trodden footpaths push their way through the brambles and bracken.

Below us, the beach, with its wide dunes, creates a landscape that contrasts dramatically with the flat sweep of the sand as it runs away to the tide. I've always enjoyed sand dune landscapes: soft sand between the toes, gazing out to sea, watching the early morning sun rising up from the horizon line, always seems to hold promise. Solitude and contemplation heighten the anticipation; what might this precious day bring?

A small flock of gannets in the distance drops from the air into the grey green waters onto a shoal of fish. Seagulls screech overhead. The last wisps of morning sea mist are slowly lifting. Out to sea, a patch of silver light on the water promises a little brightness to come. The glorious, hot sunny summer this year has almost imperceptibly given way to a mellow, misty autumn.

As I watch, the mist starts to dissolve and a scrap of sunlight begins to spread in from the sea, breathing new life into the bracken; now a deep glowing gold. The gaudy yellow of the autumn-flowering gorse bushes gives off an almost fluorescent glow.

The white dots of sheep are spread out over the distant fields to the far left of the beach. They're grazing among fresh, pale green bracken where the field meets the rolling hills; where we walked yesterday up and along the coastal path from Widemouth to Bude.

★ ★ ★

I remembered that we had walked those paths earlier in the year. Then the warmth of a glorious May day had evaporated and the sea mist crept up the valley. There was a bank on the far side of the road covered with delicate, late flowering primroses, still bright yellow in the lengthening evening shadows.

I compared the surroundings then and now: an early morning in late September now; an early evening in May then. Both landscapes unrivalled, both full of pleasures that can't be bought.

★ ★ ★

We walk down onto the beach where the incessant crash of the waves grows louder. The tide is on the turn and rushes up between the rocks at each roll in, depositing its cargo of seaweed onto the shore before receding to form again the swell of the next wave.

There is such inevitability about the tide that all uncertainties appear diminished by its relentless to and fro. Whatever happens in rapidly changing or uncertain times, the tide will turn, and the sun will rise.

I throw one last ball along the beach for Harriet, before heading back to climb the dunes. My step is determined and my confidence strengthened by the timelessness of our sojourn. I pop into the village shop, before it's really open, to get some still-warm croissants to take back for us all for breakfast. Aren't I the lucky one to have grown-up children who still want to include Harriet and me in their holidays? The warmth of our breakfast comes through the white paper bag onto my hands, reminding me of the secret treasures I'm bringing back for them.

★ ★ ★

HELEN

The thought of secrets makes me think of many confidences the district nurses shared and always carried with them.

On one particular morning, I was passing a house that, several weeks ago, I had been attending daily, and I began wondering how things were in the family now. I had visited to dress a wound on a young child, where a burn had been caused by him tipping very hot coffee over himself. It had healed well and it was some time now since I'd finished visiting. I'm not sure what made me stop and knock on the door, but I had become used over the years to following my intuition when it seemed to nudge me. It wouldn't take a minute just to pop in and say hi.

Helen answered the door and welcomed me in, announcing that it was a good time to call because Joe, the little one, was down for his sleep and she was just going to have coffee. Why did I feel something unspoken was hanging in the air? Maybe it wasn't really a good time to call after all... Helen continued on, almost hurriedly, as she made the drinks; wiping down kitchen surfaces and chattering too rapidly. There was a lovely homemade cake sitting on the kitchen table, with a big layer of bright blue butter icing on top, forked up into peaks. Helen seemed to hesitate as she handed me my coffee and, to my surprise, I noticed tears beginning to roll down her cheeks. She caught her breath as she blurted out that, somewhere, there was a little boy who was seven today and she didn't even know whether or not he was alive.

Helen had given birth to her first baby when she was just sixteen years old in a 'naughty-girls-home' in North London, handing the baby over for adoption at six weeks old. Her parents had disowned her at the time they discovered she was pregnant. Helen had never managed to tell her husband about her illegitimate son. Every year on his birthday she made her firstborn a cake.

I'm pleased to be part of a society that no longer condemns women in Helen's position to suffer this perpetual cruelty; a sorrow without relief, that doesn't ease, where the pain, the guilt and the heartache go on throughout their lives with no reprieve. There is no end to the sentence they are forced to serve for their perceived crime.

I remember thinking about the memory boxes and scrapbooks that I used to help parents put together when they were dying, to leave for their children. Some would write letters for their children to read when they were perhaps eighteen, expressing their love. Some left photos, or diary accounts of special days; and I knew how precious these mementos become to children whose parents have died.

I wished Helen had been able to write a letter or leave a keepsake for her baby, so that he would know how much she loved him.

★ ★ ★

I quicken my step in an attempt to leave my thoughts behind, as Harriet and I begin climbing the hill back to the chalet. Harriet shows some reluctance to go back but I manage to convince her that we will return tomorrow. She seems to get the message and remembers she'll get breakfast when we get back. We're nearly there at the cabin and everywhere is still and quiet. I can only just hear the now distant waves breaking on the sand. It must be nearly high tide now.

13

DISTANCE LENDS
ENCHANTMENT TO THE VIEW

Harriet is excited today as we start a new walk along a canal bank. I've come over to walk with Kay, a very dear work colleague. She is twenty years younger than me and so still there on the district as a community nurse or, as she informs me now, an 'Adult Community Care Worker'! We worked in partnership for several years, sharing the same caseload. We worked well together and Kay was one of the few features of the job I was sorry to leave by the time I retired. It was a good partnership that she was sorry to lose too. We held shared beliefs about what good nursing care was and, together, managed to continue to spend more of our time concerned with patients, rather than computers.

In some sense, being from the 'old school', I had managed to hold back some of the constant continuous changes that were being forced on us; not all of them by any means but I continued working closely as a team member with the GPs for many of my latter years. This allowed us continuity of patient care even though that was rapidly being pulled apart in the name of progress by nursing management.

I listen to Kay as we talk about what's happening now and my heart bleeds for the care that has disappeared and I feel sad that her care-giving abilities are now unappreciated, even unrecognised, in this climate of 'never mind the quality; it's only the quantity of visits that counts'.

It's a lovely day, with just a hint that summer might be on its way, borne out by blossom fluttering at the far end of a rather scraggy branch

*overhanging the canal. The boats tethered alongside our path bob up and
down in the water, as other barges pass by. Some are clearly inhabited, with
gingham curtains and window boxes, while others seem forlorn and deserted.*

*It's great to see Kay. Many work acquaintances fall away when work
terminates, and you find that the only thing you shared was the job. I feel
fortunate that this friendship has continued, has in fact grown stronger, since
I left. Kay throws yet another stick for Harriet along the towpath and we go
on to talk about how much a part of my life Harriet has become. It's strange
how the years between Kay and myself disappear. She tells me she thinks
I've made a great job of retiring and goes on to say she thinks I've really
embraced retirement like no-one else she knows. We give each other a hug
and arrange to meet for lunch in a couple of weeks' time. Harriet decides
she'd like to stay longer and hesitates before getting up onto the back seat of
the car. She then stares longingly out of the back window as I pull away with
a goodbye wave to Kay. I'm glad it's not long until we get together again; we
always have more to say. She's only about ten years older than my kids and
I'm certainly nearer her mother's age than that and yet we relate as friends; a
special friend who's seen me go through the end of my career and into
retirement and who shared that very special retirement party with me.*

★ ★ ★

As I drive home, I'm giving thanks again for all those blessed
friendships. I'm thinking about how I've adapted to retirement
and how it has felt for me and how great it is. I have a number of
other friends who see leaving work as the end of everything;
whereas for me it has felt more like the beginning of something
else. When I was pregnant with my first child, and leaving my
district nurse/midwife post that had always been my career goal,
friends said then what they also said when I was retiring:

"You'll never leave. You'll be back in months. Nursing is in
your blood; you'll never manage without it!"

Yet I never hankered to return to work. I've always been
pleased that I had the opportunity in those early years to be a stay-

at-home mum. It was a different career, another beginning, and I still see it as the principal and most valuable job I did. To have to return to full-time nursing at the time of the divorce, with my youngest aged only six, was painful for me.

I worked from home in a small way throughout those years with a young family, teaching antenatal classes; to prepare couples for childbirth.

It was something I got great satisfaction from; something I felt was a service I was able to provide and provide well. Making it possible for parents to have a meaningful labour experience kept me close to the midwifery I loved and enabled me to give care in a way that brought its own rewards. It also opened my mind to teaching; an ability I developed and took pleasure in returning to much later in my career.

My working life has grown up around those two big life events it seems: birthing and dying. Whether caring for, or teaching about; these life events have been at the heart of my career and for by far the largest part, set within the community in which I've lived. I'm wondering why this has been the direction I've taken within my vocation, when it occurs to me that these are situations where the full theatre of life is played out; emotional places, sorrowful and joyful places. Have I sought these settings in which to work or have they sought me out; do they use some hidden ability within me or am I drawn to the struggle for survival that surfaces in all who become caught up in these experiences? I'm left wondering, with no answers; perhaps there aren't any.

Retirement throws up different thoughts. Perhaps we're more inclined to think of retirement as an end, rather than a new beginning, whereas, essentially, it *is* a new beginning... a start of growing old, perhaps.

Maybe that's the big difference. Each generation will have longer lives than their parents and yet the society in which they will experience that longer life almost forbids them to grow old, requiring that they remain young for as long as possible. Ageism is unbridled in our youth-orientated society. We expect the elderly to disappear and be content with the crumbs we throw them. With this attitude, it's little wonder that when they are made to feel in the way, so many become withdrawn and feel they are no longer worth anything. I was always perturbed as to why, when we admitted retired persons into hospital, we always referred to what their job had been when they were working. It was always *retired* shopkeeper or *retired* builder. Why don't we ask what they do *now*, rather than what they did *then*? It all goes to emphasise that what they did then was important but what they do now isn't. The older we become, the more we are seen as burdensome. So maybe it isn't surprising that so many of us fear getting older and consequently don't perceive retirement as a new beginning or a journey to look forward to.

Yet I really believe it is possible to live to old age retaining self-esteem, growing old positively, feeling fulfilled, and living harmoniously with rich friendships. Retirement would seem to offer a good opportunity to start getting a feel for it; planning to grow old well. We are surrounded by suggestions for keeping physically healthy but living a contented, well-balanced life may be more to do with the psychological and spiritual aspects of our lives.

Being happy in retirement has to surely be the forerunner to being happy in old age. Equally, it is perhaps personality differences that define our retirement behaviours. Maybe the 'glass half full' temperament, rather than the 'glass half empty' characteristic, encourages a happier, more positive, approach to growing old. For me, it's become a time of freedom, with more time to myself and with less to worry about.

There is an inner place of stillness that has found somewhere to settle inside me; it's a feeling of contemplation, almost akin to meditation, I think. It's a place I want my spirit to hold on to always because it somehow recognises the precariousness of life without exposing fear about what might happen next; bringing about an acceptance that what will be will be. Maybe that is part of growing older; I have indeed seen serenity in some older people, some with a certain presence that seems to sing out contentment. These times encourage in me a feeling of being essentially a castaway, here in my stillness.

As I arrive home, still thinking about my lovely walk with Kay, I decide to top up my 'glass half full' attitude to life by pouring some Merlot into a rather nice glass, one of a precious set given to me when I retired by a very special lecturing colleague. I determinedly fill the glass, not only half but right to the brim, as I wonder how much being happy in retirement has to do with being happy to be alone; happily being single.

Conceivably, a leaflet entitled 'Keeping Happy in Retirement' might be more useful than the 'Keeping Fit' one; after all, managing our psycho-spiritual selves has to be at least as important as the 'eat less, exercise more' advice.

★ ★ ★

We're taking a late walk today, right up the hill to the farm. We've already done about five miles. It's been a beautiful day and it's now late afternoon and the heat of the day has gone. A gust of wind ruffles Harriet's fur as she tears ahead and I follow on up the path by the hedge, climbing slowly to the top, glad of that breeze on my face. I stand and turn, looking down the hill, and cast my eyes all the way round, feeding them with the scene.

It's one of those blissful moments when everything feels right with the world; when the sheer good fortune of being here and being me for this one moment in time seems to flood my heart with joy and contentment. Summer's riches will not last. I breathe in deeply, trying to draw something from the instant and lock it within me forever. I can almost taste the coming together of it all; the sweet smell of new mown grass, the low hum of bees in the hedge blossom, the pale warmth of the evening sun. And here am I, as part of the setting, a woman and her dog in happy harmony.

★ ★ ★

As I negotiate the stile, I think about our local walks throughout the neighbourhood, and the miles we have covered in all directions, in all weathers. We have ambled through meadows, strolled through woods, stepped purposefully along roadsides, criss-crossing the well-trodden footpaths across the landscape with our two feet and four paws marking out our very own patchwork territory. (There was often some other 'marking' undertaken by Harriet but let's not blight the image.)

The unravelled garment of my life seemed to knit together on those blessed walks – the plain and the purl, the joy and the care – the walks gave me the opportunity to recognise the colours and the pattern.

These times and reflections have been a gift; a precious gift from Harriet. The nature of our relationship moves on with every day and every walk. I feel she has accompanied me on my reflective journey into my past, and she's now with me moving forward to my future. She provides a very real companionship, not a replacement for human connections but a steadfast and loving presence; these are gifts I could never repay.

★ ★ ★

I return my gaze to my present. The intensity of the daylight is just beginning to fade, but the sheep grazing on rolling pasture behind and to my left are still visible. I have a newfound fondness for sheep that has developed alongside my passion for sheepherding. Their presence adds an enduring timelessness to the country scene.

★ ★ ★

I allow my mind to take a flight of fancy, wondering whether to risk adding to my perfect life by seeking out the farmer to see whether he would allow us to practise our sheepherding skills on some of his sheep. Could there be anything more perfect right now than having Harriet go to the end of that field at my behest and bring those sheep to me on this beautiful day? I'll never be able to have my own herd of sheep in my very own field but maybe there is a farmer somewhere who would be delighted to have us work his sheep. I'm imagining we would move them leisurely from field to barn with Harriet performing brilliantly.

I then remember her attempted execution of the outrun and lift in our sheepherding session this week; and realise perhaps we're not quite ready… and would the farmer appreciate that my interest is only in his sheep?

I reflect on my contentedness with my single life; with Harriet as my significant other. I remember the words of the feminist Germaine Greer, when she talked of the release from the continual need and insatiable desire for sex that accompanies the ageing process; and so it is… well, most of the time.

I find now that I really do like this single life. Alongside its shortcomings, there seem to be a host of compensations that are just *there*, that don't have to be struggled for or earned or negotiated; they just happen. Furthermore, they seem to be the things that many of my friends are searching for, as they face the prospect of spending retirement with their husband.

I have a freedom in my home, whilst some friends feel they are losing the freedom in theirs, with husbands retiring and seeming to be about the place most of the time, wanting food in the middle of the day.

"I married him for better or worse but not for lunch," a friend said recently when she'd escaped to mine for coffee. She went on to explain that her friends were more reluctant to call in when they have free time now because of husband being around. It feels, as friends talk, that their independence somehow seems to be curtailed when husband retires. Their 'space' in the home, to use at will when they leave work – maybe having a lazy day, reading a book or listening to the afternoon play on the radio –

seems to disappear. Juggling that loss alongside retirement, while 'gaining' a full-time husband, who himself is experiencing the loss of job and often status, can, it seems, prove difficult for some.

After a bad marriage, solitude can be a welcome gift. Yet it seems that many women simply have to find another partner, cannot be alone at all and often rush headlong into any relationship to save being alone; appearing to feel only half a person without a partner. For the rest of us, the damage left after divorce takes time to repair; injury is deep and healing is slow. This in itself can cause problems in other relationships that we try to develop. If you've been continually disapproved of, it's easy to misinterpret an ordinary question from someone new, to take it as criticism and to react defensively to a simple enquiry. Question: "Why have you ordered that off the menu?" Defensive Answer: "What's wrong with that as a choice?!"

Having been constantly made to feel that I didn't sufficiently financially contribute to the household budget, I became ridiculously insistent about paying my way in new liaisons. I had known a really kind, considerate man for some six months or so when he asked if I would go on holiday with him. I answered saying that I would love to as long as I paid my own way. His reply was that he had hoped for more than a week in a caravan in Wales; he wanted to take me somewhere warm and exotic. At least he understood the limits of my bank balance. But I *had* to pay my way. It felt important, even though it probably wasn't in the overall scheme of things.

Wounds may appear healed, but we take scars into those new relationships; healed wounds, yes, but with hidden bruises that remain painful when pressure is applied, so moving away from anything that may possibly rub against the sore surface becomes a pattern of behaviour. It's a precedent that can seem almost impossible to change and one that certainly exerts undeserved tension in any new association.

In today's society, many people fear being alone and are afraid of their own company and yet for me, being alone is not being lonely. It is only by being alone that I have really got to know myself. Being alone has given me the opportunity to develop companionship with myself. It has allowed me time to think and to find in myself a true friend. I now believe that taking the time and space to establish this friendship is probably the most important relationship we can ever make. It's almost certainly essential to make friends with yourself before you're ready to live with someone else. Any close friendship takes time; making friends with oneself has to be tied up with this freedom to be alone and to think.

This liberty seems to be too terrifying for many to contemplate. It appears that many older women stay trapped in stultifying relationships because to do anything else has become too scary to consider.

It has been a surprise to me to discover the joys of living alone and of treating myself sometimes. It really is great to indulge myself, perhaps by buying a ridiculously extravagant, expensive face cream or ignoring household chores in favour of spending a day at a sheepdog trial; and, best of all, to return from a chilly dog walk and have a bath, right in the middle of the day, using every drop of the hot water, just because I feel like it! I find I've learned to nurture myself; to create ceremonies of personal pleasure that feed my inner spirit. Moreover, I've realised that the presents I buy myself are wonderful – no disappointments – it's always exactly what I want! If I buy myself flowers, they are gorgeous; no nasty garage bunch of ragged carnations, but rather a beautiful spray of freesias.

There is also the release from any of those household chores that you really dislike. I revel in the joy of never needing to cook again. To be able to just look in the fridge to see what's there, to take a plate of grapes and add a few chunks of tasty cheese and to know that's it: done and dusted, meal prepared. What freedom.

No saucepans to wash, no cooker to clean, and much less shopping to do; I love it. Perhaps more expected, but nonetheless pleasing, is the uninterrupted possession of the remote control. (Unless I need to reclaim it from beneath a rucumbent Harriet taking up most of the sofa.)

Obviously there is a downside to living alone... there's always a downside. As well as the probable financial constraints, when you live on your own there is no-one to hassle you, to remind you, just by being there, that the place is untidy or that the bed is left unmade. There is only you to set the limits, to exert your own controls on how much you eat or drink, or how lazy you allow yourself to become; and then, of course, there's always the bins to put out.

The truly happy, single person is not someone who is unable to make relationships, but rather someone who possesses the talent to live alone; who can reach out to others, but who doesn't depend on others to make themselves whole or happy.

But – and it is quite a big but – I think the more time I spend alone, the less likely I am to want to grow an intimate attachment. I now have a lot to lose; not least that 'thinking space' that I would need to surrender if I had to consider the demands of a live-in partner. Maybe I've just become selfish while living alone.

A dog-person friend has also warned me against trying to get any man you may want in your life to truly like your dog. She reckons it doesn't really work; that you can push them together as much or as often as you like, and while at times it feels fine, there are other times when it appears they have an emotional distance from your dog that you don't. She says they sort of try but don't always understand how much you miss your dog and why you don't really want to holiday without your four-legged friend. They may see faults that you don't. Probably, they disapprove of the dog being allowed on the sofa or that you feed him your crusts. (I decided not to ask whether it was the dog or her new man that she fed with her crusts.)

That's not been a problem I've come across as yet, although the facts sound plausible. Even so, somehow the relationships I have found myself in in later years have left me wanting and I have yearned for the ease of aloneness again. The complications and concessions of a live-in partnership seem to require more staying power and compromise than I want to manage anymore.

However; should the need arise, the hotel with the four-poster bed is still there and they still serve that crème brûlée.

★ ★ ★

Harriet returns to drop the umpteenth stick at my feet. We begin the walk home. She jumps up with her front paws on the top edge of the water tank in the corner of the field. She dips her head and gulps the rainwater within and then scampers off ahead with a long pink tongue dripping from the side of her mouth as she flings herself down in a dense patch of succulent-looking grass and rolls over and back, before jumping straight up onto all four paws, then dropping suddenly to a crouch before hurtling herself up into my arms with the sheer joy of the moment… Harriet knows how to live life well. I stagger as I struggle to regain my balance, laughing as I hug her close and look back over the view, grasping one more glance to feed my soul; another memory harvested to hold forever. As I weave my way through the lychgate, I quicken my pace to catch up with Harriet.

★ ★ ★

I now find I live much of my life in my head; not simply with memories, but with thoughts and feelings. Maybe it's an inevitable effect of living alone. Even when I've been away from my life, it seems always to have been there waiting for me to return. It's as though, revisiting it, I've been able to catch-up and stride alongside it comfortably, rather than constantly dodging paths where I knew difficult terrain might be.

★ ★ ★

I realise the light is fading fast; the sun has almost set behind me. Much like my life, it would seem one must wait until the evening to see how glorious the day has been. The sunset has left behind a vivid red sky on the horizon – 'a shepherd's delight' – and, with it, the promise of a great tomorrow.

Harriet turns and scampers playfully back to meet me. I lean down and ruffle the dishevelled fur that comes down over her eyes, silently inviting her to 'Come along; grow old with me… the best is yet to be'.

★ ★ ★

THE END

ACKNOWLEDGEMENTS

I want to thank John Martin for his delightful pen and ink sketches. He captures Harriet so well.

I very tentatively submitted my very first draft to Jan Moran Neil who not only offered me valuable feedback but, more importantly, inspired me. Without her belief in my writing ability, I'm not sure this book would have been born.

The understanding of where I found myself at the time of my divorce, sensitively displayed by Elke Dutton in her poem, reflects the close friendship we shared at that time. I will always be grateful for her sincere portrayal of my feelings.

Thanks must go to Di Lord who always believed I had something significant to say and who strives, against so many odds, to keep the art of nursing at the heart of her patient care.

To Kathy Nelson, my friend and fellow author, thank you for being instrumental in re-energising me to push forward with publishing. Your interest in my writing has meant so much.

A big thank you goes to many friends for all their support; many of whom, like me, fear the demise of the caring art of nursing. So many of you gave time to reading excerpts, making suggestions and encouraging me with your enthusiasm for the message I was struggling to convey in the text.

Thank you to all the patients and families I was privileged to serve who allowed me to share very emotive, memorable times with them and who taught me so much.

The love of my children Jon, Ben, Matt and Izzie is a treasured gift; a gift beyond measure, unceasingly given. Thank you is so not enough.

VISIT THE AUTHOR'S WEBSITE:

www.dinahlatham.co.uk

THE QUEEN'S
NURSING INSTITUTE

The Queen's Nursing Institute is a registered charity dedicated to improving the nursing care of people in their own homes. They trained district nurses until the 1960s in a model that was copied across the world. Today, the charity carries out a wide range of functions supporting nurses and their patients in the community through educational grants, professional networks, publications, research and events. It works with nurses in an effort to ensure that good quality community nursing is available to everyone where and when they need it. To find out more about the charity's work and perhaps make a donation, please visit their website at www.qni.org.uk.